THE GOSPEL ACCORDING TO FIRST GRADE

Other books by Patricia Ann Fisher

Gingerbread Girl
Lord, Don't Let It Rain at Recess
Lord, Don't Let It Rain at Lunch

THE GOSPEL ACCORDING TO FIRST GRADE

Humorous Devotions for Teachers (and Others) Who Nurture the Dreams of Children

PATRICIA ANN FISHER

ZondervanPublishingHouse
Grand Rapids, Michigan

A Division of HarperCollinsPublishers

The Gospel According to First Grade
Copyright © 1995 by Patricia Ann Fisher

Requests for information should be addressed to:
    Zondervan Publishing House
    Grand Rapids, Michigan 49530

Library of Congress Cataloging-in-Publication Data

Fisher, Patricia Ann.
    The gospel according to first grade : humorous devotions for
teachers (and others) who nurture the dreams of children / Patricia
Ann Fisher.
       p.   cm.
    ISBN: 0-310-50061-3 (softcover)
    1. Elementary school teachers—Prayer—books and devotions—
English. 2. Christian life. I. Title.
BV4596.T43F564   1995
242'.68—dc20   95-5357
                                                    CIP

Edited by Mary McCormick
Interior design by Sherri L. Hoffman

Printed in the United States of America

95 96 97 98 99 00 / ❖ DH / 10 9 8 7 6 5 4 3

Dedicated to
Jamie, Leslie, Michael, Matthew,
and the new little one
and
My editor, Mary McCormick,
and
To Jim, without whom my writing
would never have happened.
With love always. Thirty years is
just the beginning.

This service that you perform is not only supplying the needs of God's people but is also overflowing in many expressions of thanks to God.

2 Corinthians 9:12

Contents

Acknowledgments

I would like to thank the many people who encouraged and assisted me with *The Gospel According to First Grade*: Joyce Ondersma, Lyn Cryderman, Mary McCormick, Scott Bolinder, Stanley Gundry, Dr. Wayne Rood, Elinor Raymond, Debby Goehring, and the congregation of St. John's. A special thanks to Jim and Amanda for enduring and assisting in the book-writing process with humor and grace.

Overture

A teacher has a mission, a calling to serve the Lord. I believe that strongly. At the same time, she's usually a nurse, a counselor, a substitute mom (or dad if she's a he), a cheerleader, a disciplinarian, a Sunday school teacher, and a community leader. At home she's frequently a real mom (or dad), a chauffeur, a cook, a window washer, a laundress, a dishwasher, a cleaning lady, and the spiritual head of the family.

She's still determined about her mission when it's below zero with a blizzard on the way and the car won't start and school begins in thirty minutes. A teacher continues to be resolute and caring of others even when her own five children all have chicken pox and even the pediatrician has sent a get-well card.

A teacher is still undaunted when the water heater explodes and her house is under a foot of water and the pool collapses because of the last earthquake. She still has her vision and dreams when the kids at home paint a mural on the new wallpaper, the cat has eight kittens in spite of a visit to the vet, and half the class at school also has chicken pox while the other half is waiting to get it. She's still hanging in when the washing machine is burping pink bubbles from the laundry room into the kitchen and the refrigerator defrosts the gourmet meal she's serving to her husband's boss from Toledo.

It's for teachers like these that this book is written—teachers who, in the face of overwhelming obstacles, continue to care about the children they teach.

For, as teachers, we have this ministry and have no time for less than the best. We have this ministry in the toughest of times. We have this ministry so we shall not lose heart. We have this ministry so we'll keep the faith and continue to pass it on, intact, to others. We have this ministry because we always expect the finest. We have this ministry so we always find time to share the Gospel. Even when we cannot speak the words, we know that our actions had better count because that's all there's going to be. *The Gospel According to First Grade* (or second or third or high school or whatever you teach), shares some accounts of how the gospel works within us. We cannot read chapters or demand memory verses, but we can proclaim the Word by who we are and what we do. It's not easy, but we *can* do it with the Lord's help.

BEGINNING THE JOURNEY

It's the first day of school. I've been awake most of the night with butterflies of anticipation. After all, I'm setting out on a 185-day voyage, and there is much to think about.

For the past week I've worked tirelessly in my classroom to ensure the success of this day. There are colorful, newly designed bulletin boards and bright banners welcoming the children to first grade. All the books have been distributed and placed in newly scrubbed desks. On each desk is a carefully lettered name tag for the child who is to sit there. Each moment of the day has been structured to ensure that a clear message is portrayed: *This is a place for learning, a place to dream, to achieve, a place of love and concern, a place of expectation.* A teacher has an opportunity on the first day of school that she will never have again, a time to create an anticipation of great happenings, a time to share the enthusiasm of learning, and a time to set the limits of behavior.

The alarm screams. I rush to turn it off and after a speedy shower quickly dress in my new back-to-school outfit. In the kitchen, Amanda, my youngest daughter, is already gobbling cereal. She's crisply dressed in a new jeans skirt, snowy white shirt, and a jeans vest worn casually open.

"Hi, Mom," she grins as I give her a quick hug. "This is the day that you get that really awful class, isn't it?"

"That's their reputation," I admit, and I begin to wonder if I can help this class achieve the inner control that makes learning possible. Every teacher has a quiet corner of fear that she may be unable to teach a class, particularly a class that already may have a reputation for being difficult.

As I arrive at school, I carefully sweep away that corner of doubt, and the expectation of joy prevails as I walk to the playground to meet my new first graders. I'm not in a hurry to take them indoors. Instead, I inspect the line of children, offering encouragement to those who are in line quietly. "What a wonderful line," I tell them. "And you all have such super smiles. We're going to do so many terrific things in first grade." I am setting the stage.

They grin back. In the months to come they'll learn to read, learn to count, learn to write, as well as learn more about the world around them. They'll lose teeth, tie their own shoes, and take giant leaps toward self-sufficiency.

My heart sings in anticipation. Now it's time to share the song.

Lord, help me to listen more and to speak less. Help me to encourage lavishly and to always expect the best. Help me to share Your love even when I cannot speak of it. Lord, help me to hear the lyrics of this new first grade. Help my classroom to grow into a symphony of love. Amen.

And whatever you do, whether in word or deed, do it all in the name of the Lord Jesus, giving thanks to God the Father through him. COLOSSIANS 3:17

GOOD MORNING,
MRS. FISHERMAN

There was a time very long ago when I was grateful for having a simple last name. After all, "Fisher" isn't difficult to pronounce—even a first grader should have no problem learning my last name. That turned out to be a wildly optimistic assumption.

I tell my class on the first day of school, "My name is Mrs. Fisher." They nod. Then I write it on the board. They squint their eyes, trying to understand the correlation between those chalk marks and my name.

Even though I leave my name at the top of the chalkboard and remind the children of it frequently, I am not at all surprised when Joseph says, "Mrs. Fisherman, may I use the unifix cubes?"

"Oh, Mrs. Fish, I have to go the bathroom so bad," Kenisha steams, her brow furrowing against her café-au-lait skin, her dark eyes pleading.

"Did you forget that we have bathroom passes and that you don't have to ask?" I remind her. There's no time for another lesson on my name at that point.

"I forgot," she says as she grabs the pass and runs out into the hallway in a frenetic gallop.

"Oh, Mrs. Fisherman, I love your shoes," comments Melanie as she pats them at story time while I'm sitting on the beanbag.

Then Jenny reaches up to hold my hand as we walk to the playground for recess. "I love you, Mrs. Fish," she says as she skips along, taking me with her.

And I recall a long time ago when I was in first grade and the principal's name was Mr. Littlejohn but Mr. Littlejohn wasn't little at all, and I still remember how much that puzzled me. I tried so hard to learn his name. One day I courageously approached him. "Good morning, little Mr. Bigjohn," I said and then blushed to my fingertips as he threw back his head and laughed uproariously.

So I try tender, loving care for my little ones, knowing that learning names sometimes takes awhile.

Our Father, I thank You for the knowledge that You know us and love us by name. Help me likewise to know and love these little ones I teach. Amen.

"Whoever welcomes one of these little children in my name welcomes me. . . ." MARK 9:37

D'ELEGANCE

On the Saturday following the first week of school, several teachers from Adams School meet for lunch at a restaurant called D'Elegance. Locals, not given to elaborate names, simply call it "Del's." It's time for one final tribute to summer, a time to don bright Sunday-best cottons perhaps for the last time before cooler weather beckons.

D'Elegance is a restored Victorian mansion nestled in a grove of valley oak trees that spread their branches protectively around it. Inside, the rooms are individually decorated with green plants, antiques, floral wallpaper, and softly burnished brass. In one room there is a fireplace for cozy wintry days and a large, octagonal stained-glass window. In another there's a harp for soft dinner music. In the place we've chosen is a spacious porch overlooking a flower garden. In the distance are the soothing sounds of a gurgling waterfall spilling to a river below.

Shelly, my best friend on the faculty, and another first grade teacher, and I are the first to arrive. As we are seated, we quietly comment on the beauty and tranquillity of the setting, much welcomed after the pace of the first week of school.

Olivia, tall, slim, with snowy-white hair pulled softly away from her face, soon joins us. She had talked of retirement a couple of years ago, but now her face alights with excitement as she begins to recount the challenges of her new sixth graders.

Mary Ann, our second grade teacher, and Marty, who teaches kindergarten, arrive next. Mary Ann, her brown skin setting off large, expressive dark eyes, a soft Afro framing her face, smiles jokingly, "I'm here; we can eat." Mary Ann loves all food as long as there's enough of it.

Marty, who teaches kindergarten, laughs lightly at Mary Ann, as she peers over the porch railing at the garden before pulling up a chair. Her long, dark tresses have been shorn this summer into a short, black cap of natural curls.

Only Maggie, who teaches third grade, is not here. She has been at school on time for the past couple of years, but before that she'd usually struggle in a few days or a few weeks late. Maggie has taught at Adams School for as long as anyone, including her, can remember. She's a free spirit; around Maggie there are always surprises.

"Maggie called me last night," Olivia begins. "She's been in Scotland most of the summer but then decided to do some white-water rafting in Colorado with her daughter. 'I just forgot my calendar, and it didn't seem time for school to begin yet until Susan, my daughter, reminded me,' she said," Olivia recounts. "She'll be here Tuesday or Wednesday," Olivia finishes.

"Shall I remove the extra chair," a waitress offers, "since the other lady won't be here?"

"No," we reply in near-unison. For whether or not Maggie is here in person, we all feel her presence still.

When we've all eaten our favorite lunch—D'Elegance Delight, a generous sampling each of salmon, shrimp, and chicken salad served on a bed of French spring greens with crusty rolls—the waitress returns with a tray of desserts.

"Oh, nothing for me," Shelly protests while the rest of us nod in agreement. It's too soon to abandon our summer diets.

"These desserts are compliments of a lady named Maggie who called this morning," she explains as she places large pieces of D'Elegance mud pies before us. The waitress continues, "It's made of mocha and chocolate ice cream and layered with fudge and peanut butter on a chocolate-cookie macadamia nut crust. "You'll love it," she smiles. "Everyone does."

We all stare wistfully at the empty chair. "Eat up, girls. That's what Maggie would say," Marty smiles as she lifts her fork in a salute.

"Farewell, diet, until a better time," Mary Ann agrees, sighing with pleasure at the first bite.

Even in her absence, Maggie has made the day!

Lord, keep Maggie in Your care. Thank You for the blessing her life and good humor are to the rest of us as she marches to a drummer the rest of us do not hear. Bless each of us, too, as the new school year begins. Amen.

And I pray that you, being rooted and established in love, may have power, together with all the saints, to grasp how wide and long and high and deep is the love of Christ, and to know this love that surpasses knowledge—that you may be filled to the measure of all the fullness of God.
EPHESIANS 3:17–19

THE PERFECT CHILD

Every year I get at least one perfect child in first grade. As a newborn infant, this child slept all night, said "Mama" at two months and "Da-da" at three months. She walked at seven months and learned to read by ten months. She rode a two-wheeler at two years of age and by three was a devoted viewer of McNeil-Lehrer. By four she could play trumpet, flute, and clarinet, as well as the church organ. At five she became the assistant teacher in the kindergarten class. And now she has come to first grade.

For the first two weeks of school I didn't perceive her genius. She was treated just the same as every other first grader. Then the day came when I assigned little Tammy to read with the red reading group.

The next day Tammy's mother was soaring around the door of my classroom as I arrived at school. "You put my Tammy in the red reading group," she sputters, her eyebrows nearly merging with her hairline. "Why, she's been reading since she was ten months old," she adds indignantly.

"The reading group a child begins with doesn't mean that much," I try to explain. "There are some terrific kids in the red reading group. And children often change reading groups as the year progresses. I'd like to give Tammy a little bit of extra time to adjust to first grade. I assure you that Tammy is going to have every opportunity available to her—she's a very special little girl."

"I know that," she mutters. "But everyone knows that the blue reading group is better. Tommy Maxwell, José Gutierrez, Annie Marcus, and Emily Diaz are all in the blue group. That's where I want Tammy. Please move her today," she finishes firmly as she stalks away.

I won't change Tammy's reading group right now because in the short time I've begun to know her, I can see how insecure she is and how truly frightened of competition and possible failure. Tammy's group will be a bit slower-paced, a little less competitive. It will emphasize skills more, and best of all, it will be a place of acceptance for a little girl who has been pushed her entire life. Reading isn't about who can get there first—often my two top reading groups are at the same level by the end of the year. The path has been a little different, though. Being in the red group will take a little pressure off Tammy now in order to achieve better things in the long run.

Nevertheless, since Tammy is a perfect child, her mother will talk to the principal, then to the superintendent of schools, and, finally, will move Tammy to a private school where the teacher will be able to recognize a perfect child.

Lord, my heart aches with longing for little Tammy. And now she is gone, and so is the opportunity to reach her. All the small signs of renewed confidence and happy giggles had begun to appear. Forgive me, Father, I did not do enough. Help Tammy's new teacher to communicate the insights I could not. In Christ, Amen.

Whatever happens, conduct yourselves in a manner worthy of the gospel of Christ. PHILIPPIANS 1:27

IN THE ABSENCE OF MIRACLES

It's the second week of school. Marty, one of the kindergarten teachers, collapses on the sofa in the teacher's lounge. "I'm exhausted," she sighs. "Every year I forget just how many children are unprepared for kindergarten. Children should have some basic skills before they enter school, some readiness."

"You're asking for miracles, Marty," Shelly answers.

"Maybe ... ," Marty replies as she leans over the edge of the sofa, grabs a notebook, and recklessly tears out a piece of paper. "I'm going to make a list," she comments. "I'll call it 'Marty's miracle list.'" The first miracle would be for every child to know her own full name; well, at least her first name," she concedes.

"Then," she continues, "every child should be potty trained. Did I tell you that one child brought a box of Pampers this year?" she asks disbelievingly.

"Also, every child should be five years old by the first day of school. Many parents don't realize that they're putting their child at an unfair disadvantage with older, more mature kids," she explains.

"And wouldn't it be wonderful if every child, before coming to school, knew something about listening —even a little," she adds.

I nod in agreement. "That's quite a list, Marty," I say.

"Well, no one ever asks for modest miracles," Marty retorts.

But I know Marty. She'll struggle on, using every ounce of energy and boundless enthusiasm even in the absence of miracles. And maybe that in itself is the greatest miracle of all.

Lord, help us to recognize the miracles in our lives, for there are many. But help us also to recognize Your presence even in the absence of miracles. Amen.

Because you have seen me, you have believed; blessed are those who have not seen and yet have believed. JOHN 20:29

MAGGIE'S AMAZING GRACE

When Maggie, our third grade teacher, returned from Scotland this year, she brought her very own bagpipes along with a kilt and tam-o'-shanter. Most of the faculty at Adams School are so predictable that it's a joy to have someone around who is as spontaneous as Maggie is.

As we're lingering with Peggy's agenda at a teacher's meeting, Maggie announces, "I want to play 'Amazing Grace' at Back-to-School Night this year. I have this vision," she explains lifting her hand as if to visualize a distant dream. "I'd be standing in front of the school dressed in my kilt, playing the bagpipes as parents approach."

Peggy nods absently. "That's all right with me."

I look at Peggy incredulously, wondering why she doesn't see a problem with that. After all, we are a public school. But Peggy doesn't seem upset or apprehensive in the least.

When the night of open house arrives, there is Maggie adorned in her brightly colored plaid kilt, her burnished orange curls bouncing in rhythm with the bagpipes that are blasting forth with no recognizable tune, just a loud and very discordant noise.

Suddenly I realize why Peggy wasn't disturbed about Maggie's playing "Amazing Grace" in a public school:

There's no possibility that anyone could ever guess what music Maggie is playing.

Still, as Maggie stands there in her brilliant plaids, her tam-o'-shanter jauntily over one eye, I'm again touched by her enthusiasm, eagerness, and good humor. Once again, Maggie has risen to the occasion! And in the background I can almost hear the lingering strains of a company of bag-pipers smiling down from a heavenly parade.

Lord, thank You for Maggie's amazing grace and the blessings she brings to our world. Someday she'll join that company of heavenly bagpipers but, Lord, not too soon, not too soon. . . . Amen.

Sing and make music in your heart to the Lord, always giving thanks to God the Father for every-thing, in the name of our Lord Jesus Christ.
EPHESIANS 5:19–20

THE BACK-TO-SCHOOL NIGHTMARE

Back-to-School Night, in my mind, is roughly equivalent to having a root canal without novocaine. Although being in front of thirty children is something I find easy and natural, being in front of thirty sets of parents is an intimidating prospect.

For one thing, first grade parents never want to sit at their child's desk. The difficulty of folding a 6'4" frame into a miniature chair may have something to do with it. Yet if parents are permitted to mill about, they invariably begin to visit with each other. To curtail this, I've decided this year to award a super star to each parent who is sitting attentively at a desk or in one of the rows of extra primary chairs at the back of the room. One of the benefits of this will also be that they will be able to see my disciplinary system in action (awarding stars for good behavior and taking away stars for inappropriate behavior). I can only hope that with parents I won't have to take any stars away!

Since I only know about half the parents in the room at this stage of the year, I begin with the ones I do know. "Mrs. Elliott already has a star. Mrs. Smithstone is ready to listen. Mr. Gomez is listening. . . ." When all the parents have sheepishly settled, I begin, "The first lesson is that you can't teach someone unless you have his or her attention." They nod vehemently, still smiling.

Suddenly I realize that we're all on the same side; we're together in this business of teaching children. After that realization, everything seems easier. I whip through an imaginary day, explaining the first-grade schedule and goals. The parents seem nearly as enthusiastic as my first graders. It occurs to me that enthusiasm is like a mirror—the image we project is identical to the reflection we see in our students and their parents!

Lord, help me never to lose my enthusiasm for teaching, even when I'm most discouraged. Let me always be a reflection of Your love. Amen.

Now we see but a poor reflection as in a mirror; then we shall see face to face. Now I know in part; then I shall know fully, even as I am fully known. 1 CORINTHIANS 13:12

WILL HE MISS ANYTHING?

As I bring my class in from the playground to begin the school day, Jeff's mother follows us. When we get to the classroom, she explains, "We're going to be gone next week. It's my husband's vacation. We're going to San Francisco to visit my husband's brother, and I just wanted to check with you to see if Jeff will miss anything while we're gone."

I want to reply, "Oh, no, of course not—we'll just close the school until Jeff gets back!" Instead, I think of how that single question, "Will he miss anything?" tends to drive well-meaning and otherwise polite teachers to kicking desks and throwing books (after the parent has left, of course).

I wonder what parents think when they ask that question. Someday I'd like to reply: "We'll be starting algebra that week, we'll be reading *Julius Caesar*, we'll have a course on writing the novel, and Raffi will be doing a concert at the school. Then, of course, there will be the class field trip to Disneyland."

Instead, I smile and write out a list of work to be completed, knowing that especially in the early grades, nothing can duplicate the classroom experience. Then Jeff's mother gives me a big hug for being such an understanding teacher.

Lord, bless Jeff and his parents and watch over them while they are away from us. And thank You, Lord, for the gift of restraint—especially when I want to throw books and kick desks. Amen.

Commit your way to the Lord; trust in him and he will do this: He will make your righteousness shine like the dawn, the justice of your cause like the noonday sun. PSALM 37:5–6

THE DOG ATE MY HOMEWORK

A teacher gets many kinds of letters from parents. This year, David's mother writes to me rather frequently—I never know what will happen next in her busy and rather hectic life. So today when David approaches my desk with a new epistle, I take it and begin to read it at once.

Dear Mrs. Fisher,

Please excuse the fact that this letter is written on a paper bag but the dog ate all the paper in the house. He's really a wonderful dog—we just got him Saturday. He's part nearly everything you can think of and is quite large. We've been trying to train him to use a newspaper but we've discovered that he loves to eat newspaper. He likes the Sunday cartoons the best. I am going to call the vet today to see if he recommends some kind of food for Henry (that's the dog's name) so that he won't eat all the paper in the house. I will admit, however, that it improves the appearance of the house to have Henry consume all the newspaper and any reprieve I can get from cleaning is very much appreciated.

You sent home David's math with a note that he should finish the problems at home and that he did know how to do them but just hadn't gotten them finished. That was a relief to me because I thought that maybe he was getting behind. David loves to dawdle but I'm sure you already know that or you wouldn't have sent his math home. At home David went to work right away; it only took him ten minutes to do the problems. They were all correct, every single one of them. After he finished all the problems he left them on the kitchen table all ready to take back to school. But then this morning when David was ready to leave for school there was Henry swallowing the last of the math—he was even licking his chops! I chased that dog all over the house with a spray bottle of water trying to punish him but the front door was open and so we all had to chase him down the street. And, of course, I still had on an old terry cloth robe in spite of the fact that Ralph, my husband, gave me a new one last Christmas. It's pink and has mauve roses on it so I want to save it for the times when I'm not working in the kitchen. Nothing makes a robe look older than food stains down the front. Also, robes are so expensive these days that I feel as though I need to take care of my new one as long as possible. But back to Henry—please excuse him for eating David's homework. If you want to send more home tonight if you could just put it in a plastic bag, then Henry won't eat it. He doesn't like plastic.

Thank you,
David's Mom

A few mornings later there is another note from David's mother:

Dear Mrs. Fisher,

David is late to school today because the alarm didn't go off. I set it for 6:30 and I know there's nothing wrong with the clock because I just bought it from Haven's and they always have the best bargains on quite high quality merchandise. I know that some people think that Haven's is overpriced but the day I was in there to buy the clock they had men's silk shirts on sale for $14.99. They were as good quality as any silk shirts I've seen. I do love silk so I bought one for my husband for Christmas. I don't know how that will work out because my husband takes off his shirt at night, wads it up, and throws it in the hamper. Well, as you may know, silk has to be washed by hand and I'm afraid I'll forget it in the hamper and it will end up in my washing machine and will be ruined. So now I'm wondering how much of a great deal I got on the shirt if my husband just wears it once and then it is ruined. Also, I wonder how much of a deal I got on the clock if it doesn't work. Today I'm going to set it several times to see if it works. I'm thinking about taking both the shirt and the clock back.

David's Mom

As I finish the letter, I chuckle to myself, wondering when I'll hear the conclusion to this tale. Several mornings later, David heads to my desk with a new letter:

Dear Mrs. Fisher,

David has lost his new winter jacket. It's a size eight. You may think that's a large size for a first grader but I bought it so that he can wear it for two years. As you know, we moved here from Minnesota. When we left I gave away all of David's winter clothes because I thought California was just one big beach. After we got here I discovered that it gets cold enough for a winter coat so I had to buy a new one for David. Fortunately, I didn't have to pay for it because I did return the alarm clock and the silk shirt to Haven's. The clock didn't work half the time and I was afraid that David's father, Ralph, would throw the shirt into the hamper and wreck it. So when I got my money back I saw that the winter jackets were on sale so I bought one for David. At first I though about putting it on my credit card but then I decided that if I paid cash I'd still have some real money left to bring home McDonald's for dinner. I love shopping but I really dislike having to make dinner afterward. I'm always in such a good mood after I've been shopping that I hate to ruin it by making dinner. Actually I like to cook; it's the cleaning up afterwards that's the pain. But back to David's jacket. He and I made a list together of the places it could be. Could you please look in each of these places? Thank you.

1. The classroom
2. The boys' bathroom
3. The girls' bathroom (David wasn't actually in there but he was chasing girls after school and they ran into the bathroom)
4. The playground
5. The cafeteria
6. The office
7. The other two first grade classrooms
8. David's desk
9. The library
10. The second grades (because it is a size eight)
11. The school bus
12. The bushes in front of the school
13. Ask all the other children if they've seen it.

Please check each item as you complete it. I'll be trying to think of other places to look and will send you that list tomorrow. It makes me sick to think I gave up a new clock and a silk shirt for that jacket. (Of course, I do remember that we also got a meal from McDonald's with that money. It's a good thing we ate those hamburgers right away or we might have lost them, too!)

Thank you,
David's Mom

That evening, David's jacket turned up in his closet at home. But not before I had completed steps 1–13.

Heavenly Father, I sometimes think that letters like these are their own reward. They keep me from taking myself too seriously. Bless David and his mother and help them not to lose his jacket again! Amen.

But the fruit of the Spirit is love, joy, peace, patience, kindness, goodness, faithfulness, gentleness and self-control. GALATIANS 5:22

THE PERFECT TEACHER

The perfect teacher comes to school three weeks early after working at home all summer, designing curriculum, visual aids, bulletin boards, and big books. She's also spent the summer attending summer school as well as taking a ten-day cultural visit to the capitals of Europe.

Once at school, she adds summer materials to her extensive files carefully, making certain that everything is in compulsive order. She then constructs intricate and informative bulletin boards and interest centers. She's also sewn book bags to slip over each student's chair, with each name carefully appliquéd on them. (Perfect teachers do not permit any additions to class lists or any deletions either, for that matter.)

The perfect teacher is friendly to everyone on the faculty without being a special friend to anyone. She takes no sides on controversial issues but encourages anyone else who does express an opinion.

The perfect teacher's clothes are fastidiously tailored and carefully coordinated for her slim body. She keeps in shape by running five miles each morning and working out at the gym three times a week.

If the perfect teacher is married, she'll have two straight-A children who appear at all the proper occasions but are otherwise carefully inconspicuous. Her husband is tall and lean with well-ordered tinges of gray in his immaculate hair.

The perfect teacher loves committee work and teachers' meetings. She works very hard to understand and delineate all issues of concern to education and society at large.

The perfect teacher is a wonderful human being, but she's not very much fun. She skims the surfaces of life without experiencing the peaks or depths. She's missed something along the way—I think it's humanity. But maybe I feel that way because I'm not a perfect teacher!

Lord, be with all of us who are not perfect, and maybe You ought to be with those of us who are perfect, too. Help us all to strive to be the best we can be, reflecting the perfection of Your love and that of Your Son, our Lord Jesus Christ. Amen.

Aim for perfection, listen to my appeal, be of one mind, live in peace. 2 CORINTHIANS 13:11

I DONE IT, TEACHER

My new box of markers explodes off my table onto the floor. Jana rushes to help me pick them up.

"Teacher, I'm sorry. I done it," sobs Javier from across the room.

"That's all right, Javier," I reassure him. "It happens all the time." But then I realize that I haven't seen Javier out of his seat all morning.

Later, the books fall out of Yolanda's desk. Since she's been tilting her desk backward all morning, it's hardly surprising. "I'm sorry, Mrs. Fisher," moans Javier. "I done it."

"It's not your fault, Javier," I reply soothingly. But Javier now has my attention, and I begin to observe him more closely.

On the playground, Kenisha falls and skins both knees. She sobs relentlessly as I leave Martha, the aide, in charge and help her limp to the office and first aid. As I return to the playground, Javier is sitting on a bench, crying. "What's wrong?" I ask him.

"I hurt Kenisha. I'm so sorry," he cries.

But I was on the playground, and I know that Javier was nowhere near Kenisha when she fell. "Javier," I say as I hold his thin little shoulder. "You did not hurt Kenisha. She tripped. Accidents happen." But he's still tearful as we line up after recess.

Then Peggy, our principal, calls an all-school assembly to announce that neighbors of the school are complaining about children's trampling flower beds on the way to school as well as after school. Afterward I see Peggy with Javier at her side. "I'll bring this little man along later. He admits to trampling flowers." Javier is hiccuping large sobs beside her.

"Peggy, I need to talk to Javier first," I implore her. She nods in curt agreement.

"Javier, you don't walk to school, do you?" He shakes his head. "And the school bus unloads children in back of the school. You haven't been near the flower beds, have you, Javier?"

He mutters a soft No, as he turns his head away.

I continue to wonder what has happened in his life that makes him want to take the blame for everything—he's such a small boy to have such very large problems. I write a note to our once-in-a-while school psychologist, George, knowing that he can deal with only the most overt and violent problems and that he'll never get to Javier.

In class I resolve to give Javier every ounce of praise and attention I can manage and, for awhile, he seems better.

But then he admits to stealing Shelly's pencil supply. "He's never even been in my room," she puzzles.

I resolve to find a way to help Javier. I write a note to his mother, requesting a conference, but she doesn't come. I try to make a home visit, but no one is there.

Then as I return to school one Monday morning, I discover that Javier and his family have left suddenly for apple harvesting in Washington. Knowing how families follow the crops, I'll probably never see him again. There are tears in my eyes and a deep heaviness in my heart for a little boy named Javier. I'll remember him always.

Lord, our heavenly Father, bless Javier wherever he is. Help his new teacher to have patience, understanding, and the resources to help him. Enfold him in the comfort of Your care. Amen.

The only thing that counts is faith expressing itself through love. GALATIANS 5:6

HIS NAME IS MATTHEW

Jamie, my son, and Leslie, his wife, are expecting a baby. Thanks to the wonders of science and sonograms, they know it is a boy, but the name for this new little one is remaining elusive to them. "We just can't decide," moans Leslie over the phone. They live in Wisconsin, and I live in California, so we can't go out to lunch together to discuss it. "We know it will be Joshua or Jacob, but we don't know which," she sighs with the resignation of a mother-to-be.

"I love both those names," I tell her. I try to recall the Joshuas and Jacobs I have had in class. "It's a win-win situation as far as I'm concerned," I assure her.

The next Sunday as we arrive home from church, the phone is ringing. I rush for it, barely managing to outrun my daughter Amanda. "It's the baby, I bet," I yell in anticipation.

"Mom," Jamie begins breathlessly. "the baby arrived about half an hour ago. Les had a really hard time because the baby wasn't in the right position, but all is well now. He weighs eight pounds, and he's beautiful."

Tears of joy fill my eyes. "Are you sure Leslie's all right?" I ask.

"Yes, she's a real trouper," Jamie replies with pride.

"Which is it—Joshua or Jacob?" I ask.

"All through labor we talked. First it would be Joshua. Then it would be Jacob. On and on it went, and then he was born, and both Leslie and I looked at each other and said almost simultaneously, 'It's Matthew!' We can't explain it—we'd never even considered the name Matthew. But that is his name."

"I love the name," I tell him. I think about the Scriptures that tell us that the Lord loves us and knows us by name. And I know for sure that the Lord has already laid claim to this very new child and that Matthew will forever be His child. Suddenly, tears of longing to hold my new grandson overflow. I want to get on the next airplane, but there are thirty-two reasons I can't.

Our heavenly Father, thank You for the gift of a new grandson. Thank You for being with Leslie and Jamie and Matthew and big brother, Michael. Bless and keep us ever in Your care, for we all are Your children. Amen.

I am the good shepherd; I know my sheep and my sheep know me. JOHN 10:14

THEY'RE HERE!

L ast year, Marty, the kindergarten teacher, complained all year about her class. "I've never seen a group of children like them," she'd explained. "Teachers depend upon the good kids to be role models for others. In this class there are no good kids! They're a mess," she wailed.

What I saw of her class in the hallways certainly confirmed everything she had said. The children pushed, shoved, hollered, cried, and screamed, sometimes all at once. When other teachers saw Marty's class approaching, they'd rush for cover.

Linda, Marty's aide, said, "It must have been something in the water that year."

Every teacher has had difficult classes. In fact, nearly every class has that potential in the first days of school, but there are indeed groups of children who give every teacher a difficult time as they progress through the grades.

This fall, since I knew they were coming, I planned for every available moment. There is so much planning that I'm breathless at the pace. I can't give these children any really unstructured moments. I know that a classroom that seems free and open and cooperative and happy is, in reality, the most planned and structured of all. It's like a pattern, very closely and intricately woven together.

Only if you get close enough is it possible to see the single strands of purpose.

One day in October, Linda, the kindergarten aide, oversees my class while I'm at a meeting. She tells me later, "I couldn't believe it is the same class. How do you do it?"

"It's very difficult," I admit. "Every moment has to be planned, and still there are times when I feel that I'm making no progress at all, that no matter how hard I try I'm not going to make a difference. At the same time, I know I have to continue to try because I want so desperately to succeed. There certainly is no time to relax and enjoy the scenery," I sigh.

Although Linda's compliment feels wonderful, I know in my heart that I wish teaching didn't have to be this difficult. Like everyone else, I'd like a moment here and there to smell the roses or, at the very least, to notice they're in bloom.

Lord, help me to remember that this class especially needs generous servings of love and encouragement. I do, too. Amen.

No discipline seems pleasant at the time, but painful. Later on, however, it produces a harvest of righteousness and peace for those who have been trained by it. HEBREWS 12:11

I WISH YOU A
PENCIL SHARPENER

The pencil sharpener in my classroom is a relic. A replacement has been ordered on my requisition list every year for the past five years, to no avail. Of course, I could have purchased one myself during that time. Teachers do a lot of that, purchasing supplies and equipment from their own funds, but somehow a pencil sharpener never seemed a priority. It's the kind of thing that becomes important only when it stops working entirely. My pencil sharpener didn't do that. It merely crunched pencils, reluctantly chopping away. Since I'm usually the only one who uses it—before school starts, I sharpen all the pencils for a day and then let the children trade in broken pencils for newly sharpened ones—I merely think about getting a new one.

Then there comes a day when Christopher, a tousled blond with large blue eyes, watches me struggle to sharpen a pencil. "Mrs. Fisher, I wish you a new pencil sharpener," he smiles, observing me carefully.

Then Melody, her dark eyes flashing, adds, "We all need to pray about it. That's what we need to do. But we have to pray by ourselves. Not like in Sunday School. Everyone to your desks now. Start praying."

I think I've never had a child as commanding as Melody. I won't destroy this precious moment, so I wait for a minute, watching all those tiny heads bowed in prayer before I tinkle the bell to begin the day.

The next morning when I arrive at school, there is a gift wrapped with a bright pink bow on the center of my desk. As I unwrap it, I smile to myself. A pencil sharpener!

Later, Melody's mother says, "When I heard about all those prayers, I went right out and bought a pencil sharpener." But my first graders are the only ones who understand what a remarkable gift it is. One of life's small joys is having a pencil sharpener that works!

The greater gift, Lord, is to glimpse the faith of these little children. Thank You, Lord, for all gifts, great and small. Amen.

One generation will commend your works to another; they will tell of your mighty acts. PSALM 145:4

KISSING CLIFFORD AND THE PENCIL SHARPENER

Now that I have a new pencil sharpener, I leave it out on the top of the bookshelf by the window. The children admire it, but few of them get to use it. Long ago I discovered that the teacher should do the pencil sharpening, and I'm not about to change that opinion. It took me so long to get this pencil sharpener that it's well on its way to becoming a first-grade treasure.

Then one day I get a complaint from Mary Ann, the second grade teacher. One of the little boys in my class, Clifford, spends his recesses kissing little girls. This isn't a new complaint. The last time Shelly was on recess duty she said, "You have to stop Clifford; he causes so many problems on the playground."

"Clifford, please don't chase girls all over the playground and kiss them," I implore him after each complaint.

He stares at me with solemn dark eyes, "It's fun, Mrs. Fisher. Some of those girls just yell and yell." His eyes begin to sparkle with mischief, even as he thinks of his ventures.

At the same time I begin to think of the strange ways we assign blame to teachers. No matter how serious a child's problems are, the minute he's assigned to a certain teacher's class, the problem automatically becomes that teacher's problem. And people will say, "Just look at how many problems that teacher has," as though she had created them herself.

"Clifford, the very next time you chase girls on the playground you'll be sent to the office and you won't even get recess," I scold him.

"All right, Mrs. Fisher, I won't kiss the girls anymore," he promises reluctantly, "but could I sharpen my new pencil?" He's intent on some kind of reward for his promise of modified behavior.

"Yes, but just this once," I agree.

I turn back to the rest of the class, who have become restive during this private interchange.

"Mrs. Fisher, Mrs. Fisher," Marissa yells, "Clifford's caught in the pencil sharpener!"

I turn around. Sure enough there's Clifford, suspended from the pencil sharpener by his jeans' zipper. His face is flushed as he yanks and pulls at his zipper, his eyes filled with tears. "I'm so stuck, Mrs. Fisher," he wails loudly.

"We'll get you loose," I soothe him, hoping to avert even louder sobs. The zipper is really stuck, however, and I have to tug and tug. It's becoming increasingly evident that it's my pencil sharpener or Clifford's zipper. After all, I can't leave Clifford hanging from a pencil sharpener. With one final tug he's free and cautiously backing away as if he fears the pencil sharpener will stalk him. So much for a pencil sharpener that works!

Lord, I guess first graders and pencil sharpeners are incompatible. Help me always to know which is more important. Bless Clifford and keep him in Your care—and help me to keep him away from both girls and pencil sharpeners! Amen.

> I know what it is to be in need, and I know what it is to have plenty. I have learned the secret of being content in any and every situation, . . . whether living in plenty or in want. PHILIPPIANS 4:12

THE LINEUP

One of the tasks of a kindergarten-and-first-grade teacher is to teach children to stand in line. It's not as easy as it looks. At the beginning of the year, my line wobbles all over with small clusters of children.

"Look how well José is standing in line," I encourage. Dennis then has to get out of line to see José. "And Kenisha is doing such a good job. Her hands are at her side, and she's looking straight ahead."

"Susie is doing such a good job. And so is Martin and Lisa and Katie and Clifford. What a wonderful line!" There are proud smiles as each student waits for recognition.

Then it comes time to actually lead the line. Most teachers have the backward walk down pat. As the line proceeds, the teacher leads it like a conductor directing a symphony, while walking backward, directing each movement. But there are inherent dangers in the procedure. Mary Ann once fell into a planter while walking backward, breaking her arm. I've noticed that she now directs her class from the end of the line, something requiring equal degrees of confidence and competence. However, Mary Ann teaches second grade, so her children come to her with some semblance of expertise in the art of line standing.

But then I go to one of the leading department stores in town to get a gift, and I notice how well people stand in line awaiting gift wrap. On the way home, there is a line for tickets for a basketball game. And at the grocery store, people are lined up with shopping carts. A man graciously lets me go ahead of him in line because I have just bread and milk. No one yells or pushes or shoves. I think that every time there's a well-ordered line, there is a teacher to thank!

Lord, one of life's lessons is to get along with others, and, it seems to me, that there's no better place to start than in a line. Grant me the insights to teach these little ones self-control, patience, and concern for each other. Help them to be caring and loving—help me to be caring and loving, too. Amen.

Through him and for his name's sake, we received grace and apostleship to call people from among all the Gentiles to the obedience that comes from faith. ROMANS 1:5

THE LORD WILLIN' AND
IF THE CREEK DON'T RISE

It's not normally a creek. In fact, it's usually a restroom. But that was before Anthony waded back to the classroom, drenched from the knees down. "Teacher, I didn't do it," he wails. "The bathroom is coming out the door!"

I'll have to leave thirty-one first graders alone if I check out his story. So I send Anthony to slosh to the office; his creaking shoes echo as he disappears down the hallway.

From a teacher's perspective, first graders and bathrooms are not very compatible most of the time. There's irresistible fun to be had in restrooms. Sticking paper towels in drains and turning on the water full force is great sport. Locking doors on the stalls and then crawling out is a source of endless merriment. Then there is the good old-fashioned water fight where there aren't any rules, just lots of water. The bathroom situation is sometimes so perilous that at one school where I taught, the principal even kept lists of children who were not permitted to use the facilities. (Fortunately, teachers chose to ignore those lists.)

I have thirty-one other children to divert my attention, however, so I've nearly forgotten Anthony when Ricardo comes back from a jaunt to the restrooms and announces, "We're having a flood, Mrs. Fisher."

I look up from my position on the floor where I'm help-ing Susie and Michael construct unifix patterns. Ricardo, too, is soaking wet.

"Liz, *help*," I write as I send Ricardo to the office with a note. (School secretaries have a high tolerance for panic, and Liz is no exception.) I am soon reassured by Liz's appearance in the doorway.

"The bathrooms are all flooded," she announces, hold-ing her hand partially over her mouth to ensure privacy. "A new custodian has been hired to help Butch. The boys' bathroom flooded, and he didn't want to bother Butch, so he mixed up a batch of cement and poured it down the drain. The cement just kept disappearing, so he had to mix more and more. We're seeing the result. The only good thing is that it's nearly three o'clock," she finishes.

After school, I ask Peggy, "Will we have school tomor-row?"

"The Lord willin' and if the creek don't rise," she replies flippantly.

Lord, I know You've had a lot of experience with floods, but Noah isn't here. Please strengthen my faith—I have a feeling I'm going to need it. Amen.

So make yourself an ark of cypress wood; make rooms in it and coat it with pitch inside and out.
GENESIS 6:14

RUNNING ON EMPTY

There's a note in the office before school the next morning to announce a brief teacher's meeting before school begins. As we gather in the faculty lounge, Peggy announces, "There's a problem with the school plumbing. No one can use bathrooms, sinks, or drinking fountains today."

We exchange disbelieving looks. "But how . . . ," I begin.

Peggy interrupts briskly. "I've contacted the gas stations in the area. Each of you will receive the name of a gas station, directions, and a map."

Olivia sputters, "Tell me I'm having a nightmare. This must be April Fools' Day, isn't it?"

"This is real," Peggy continues curtly, dismissing Olivia. "If you are careful, you'll probably have to take your class to use the restrooms only two times. Most of the gas stations are within seven or eight blocks," she finishes.

Shelly steams, "Why don't we just close the school?"

The rest of us nod vehemently. No one is very eager to undertake this adventure.

"We can't close school, because we'd be out of compliance with the rest of the district," Peggy replies matter-of-factly. "This isn't as bad as you make it out to be. All you have to do is to take a little walk two times."

"And wait while thirty-two kids use the bathroom," Olivia sighs.

Ignoring her, Peggy advises, "The school will provide bottled water for each classroom, but don't let them drink too much."

"Or it's another gallop down to the gas station," Maggie adds.

Peggy nods while the rest of us exchange stricken looks. I repress an involuntary shudder.

Then the children arrive and reality hits. Our first trek to the gas station is at 9:00 A.M. Just talking about bathrooms was enough to make first graders need to use it. We walk briskly to Sam's Gas, where nearly everyone stands quietly in line although there is also some jumping from those who most urgently need to use the restrooms. I let the jumpers go first. We get back to school at 10:30.

By lunchtime everyone needs to go again. This time it is all a bit easier. After lunch there is still another jaunt to Sam's. "Are we ever going to have restrooms at our school again?" Anthony asks wistfully.

"I hope so; I hope so," I tell him.

Finally it is 3:00 P.M. It's been the longest day I can remember. At the school office, Liz informs me solemnly, "We sent twenty-seven children home to change clothes today. Not everyone could make it to the gas station."

Lord, there was never a class in college on "How to Teach Phonics Outside of Sam's Gas." Nothing ever has prepared me to be the Pied Piper to restrooms. Yet we did survive. No one was hit by a semi, entangled in the gas hose, or caught a finger in the coke machine. But any resemblance to what I did today and teaching is purely coinci-

dental. *Thank You, Lord, for leading us safely through the city's shadows to the safety of our classroom. Amen.*

As you know, we consider blessed those who have persevered. JAMES 5:11

GRANDMA AGAIN

Tricia, the middle child of our five children, is having a baby by C-section next Monday. The event is to take place at 9:00 A.M., so I tell the children in my class, "I will be late on Monday because my daughter is having a baby and I want to be there." (I'm still remembering when I had to miss little Matthew's birth a few weeks ago. But this baby will be born in this very town, and there's no way I'm going to miss it!) "I will be back as soon as the baby is born and I get to welcome him into the world," I continue, anxious to alleviate any anxieties my first graders might have. In spite of all this reassurance, they still exchange suspicious glances. One of the fears of first graders is that their teacher might leave them, and sometimes their behavior is just cause for this reasoning.

On Monday morning, Tricia has already been taken into surgery when we arrive, so we try to carry on a trivial conversation, letting meaningless words glide around the room. "How about those '49ers," Jim says to Sean, Tricia's husband.

"My team's the Redskins," Sean replies, eyeing his watch nervously.

"How about those Redskins?" Jim persists.

Sean replies, smiling absently, "If I hang on long enough, maybe they'll start winning."

We've exhausted our limit of conversation, and there is palpable relief as we adjust to silence and pacing. Time loiters around the room, lounging in the corners.

After what seems like hours, there is movement in the nursery window in front of us. Tricia's pediatrician has emerged with a husky, howling baby boy. We all jump up to the window. We laugh as little Eric, as he is to be called, looks around and his feet are inked for footprints. He somehow manages to cover himself with ink, a forecast of mud pies to come.

As the doctor brings him out, we all rush for him. Dr. James says, "The dad first," and Sean carefully holds his new little one.

I touch his downy black hair, and then Tricia's doctor is there to assure us that she is fine but resting. I leave reluctantly because there are also thirty-two first graders awaiting me.

As I enter my classroom, the children look all around. "Where's the baby?" several voices ask at once.

"He'll come to visit soon, but he's very new right now," I explain.

"Oh," they grumble with disappointment. They'd actually expected that I'd bring the baby back with me. As usual, they are full of surprises.

In a week or so I do bring Eric to visit. When they see him, they burst into a chorus of "Happy Birthday, dear Eric." I'm stunned for a moment, until I realize that indeed their chorus is appropriate. But no one over seven would ever have thought of it!

As I sit on a chair near my desk, there is quite suddenly a whole class of first graders lined up in front of me. "Is this the touching-and-seeing line?" I ask softly. They nod seriously and come forward one by one to greet Eric and to gently touch his hair.

They lined up all by themselves, I think later with pride. *They've come a few more steps in the right direction when I wasn't even noticing!*

Lord, thank You for the gift of new life in Eric. And thank You for the ever-changing and unpredictable rewards of teaching first grade. Amen.

> I will sing to the LORD, for he has been good to me. PSALM 13:6

NO ROOM AT THE INN

Last year Olivia, Maggie, Shelly, and I went to the annual teacher's convention together. We stayed at the Hilton and had a few days of rest and adventure. But this year Peggy, our principal, will not permit that. "How will I know you even go to the convention if we aren't together?" she asks us at a teacher's meeting. Peggy has a low quotient of trust.

"We went last year," Olivia asserts. "In fact, I went to even more classes than usual. And I came back rested and eager to try new ideas."

Maggie, Shelly, and I nod in agreement.

"No more arguments. We'll do it my way this year. It will be five to a room, two double beds, and a rollaway to economize," Peggy finishes.

We all moan because we know that the motel Peggy chooses will make a Motel 6 look like luxury.

The day before the convention, we load into the school van—fourteen of us plus suitcases. Once wedged in, we can only get out by unpacking the whole van.

"I can't believe this," grumbles Shelly.

"Don't move," I warn her. "When you move, my seatbelt strangles me."

"I need something out of my suitcase," Maggie mutters as she climbs over Olivia and Kate. "I brought a pie, but I packed it by mistake."

"A pie," Olivia gasps, eyes widening with disbelief. "You packed a *pie*?"

"I was in a hurry," Maggie explains as she pulls out a crushed lemon meringue pie. "I guess it's ruined," she admits as she teeters over her suitcase. "Oh help!" she yells as she falls flat into the pie.

Shelly tries to grab her and, as she moves, Maggie emerges covered with meringue while I gasp as the seatbelt begins to strangle me again.

"I don't hold out great hope for this trip," Olivia sighs as she retrieves meringue from Maggie's hair.

"Nonsense," Peggy yells from the front seat. "Let's sing! We'll start with 'I've Been Working on the Railroad.'"

"If I'd been working on a railroad, I certainly wouldn't quit to go to a teacher's convention with Peggy," quips Olivia as we launch into the song with less than eager participation.

Finally, we stop for dinner. Peggy has chosen a fruit stand this year. We're all starved, so we stock up on peaches, apples, and pears for the rest of the journey. "What I wouldn't give for a hamburger," Shelly groans.

After our fruit dinner, we pile into the van again. It's Olivia's turn to be strangled by the seatbelt while I sit on Maggie's suitcase with the lingering odor of lemon meringue. "This is sheer torture," Olivia mutters. As time passes, we are becoming more and more fatigued, with aching muscles longing for a stretch. We wish for the convention we attended last year.

Finally, we are in San Francisco. We all climb stiffly from the van as we survey the ramshackle old hotel Peggy has chosen for us. "Rooms—$14 a night" flashes before us on flickering neon lights.

"We can't stay here," I comment as I watch Peggy stride from the van into the hotel lobby. It seems that Peggy has outdone herself this year. We are literally on skid row.

But within moments, Peggy hurries from the hotel. "They lost our reservation," she huffs. "There is no room at the inn."

"Thank goodness," Olivia sighs. "Peggy, we need a decent place to stay." She is checking her motel guide. "There's a new Howard Johnson just a short distance from here," she offers.

"If you want to stay there at your own expense, that's fine," Peggy snaps. But this time she's confronting teachers who are exhausted and hungry. We all choose the Howard Johnson. To our amazement, Peggy parks the van, unloads her suitcase, and follows us in.

Father, not only am I grateful for a place to rest in peace, but I thank You, Lord, for the reassurance that Peggy is with us and not wandering alone in the city. Amen.

I will lie down and sleep in peace, for you alone,
O LORD, make me dwell in safety. PSALM 4:8

I LEFT MY HEART IN SAN FRANCISCO

As the teacher's convention concludes at noon on Saturday, Peggy says wistfully, "Someday I'm going to come back to San Francisco. I've been coming to these conventions for years, and I've never seen San Francisco—just the convention."

Maggie replies, "Let's do it now. Never put off an adventure until another day. That's my motto. No one has to be back early, does she?"

There's a chorus of no's. After all, we've been held captive in meetings for two days. We're all ready for a break.

"I'll drive," Olivia interrupts. Since we've all experienced Maggie's reckless abandon at the steering wheel, there is no disagreement.

"Fisherman's Wharf," Maggie directs Olivia. As the van laboriously climbs a steep hill, its engine groaning, we are quite suddenly at the top, where there's a breathtaking view of San Francisco Bay with the Golden Gate Bridge etched in the background. "Hang on," Maggie yells as we start down, roller-coaster style.

"This is where you understand the true meaning of 'I Left My Heart in San Francisco,'" Shelly shrieks with laughter while I'm hoping that Peggy remembered to get the van's brakes checked.

At the bottom of the hill we are suddenly enmeshed in a combination of wall-to-wall people and a traffic jam where nothing seems to move. "Over here, there's a parking building," I offer to Olivia, pointing.

Olivia turns the wheels, abruptly swerving to avoid hitting the throngs of tourists. "The part I didn't tell you," she grins," is that Maggie taught me how to drive!"

We all laugh merrily as we park and get out of the van. "Pier 39 first," Maggie begins as she leads us toward a restored wooden pier where colorful shops nestle. "There are tons of shops here. Have fun, and we'll meet back at the entrance in forty-five minutes," Maggie orders exuberantly.

Shelly and I rush for the shops, intrigued by the music boxes one shop offers, studying the variety of chocolates in another (and, of course buying some samples), stopping for cotton candy, boarding an antique merry-go-round and listening to its nostalgic tune. Then we follow the crowd to look at sea lions resting on rocks below the pier, where fishing boats used to dock. "I've heard that the sea lions moved in, and the fishing boats had to leave," I comment, as we observe the huge animals barking in vociferous conversation. With one last glance we hurry into a shop with stuffed animals, where I buy a bunny for my grandson, Matthew, and a whimsical seal for his brother, Michael. Then there's a jewelry shop twinkling with shimmering gold and gems, where Shelly buys earrings. We've just begun to survey the shops when we discover that our time is up, and we race to meet the others at the entrance.

"It's about a block to Fisherman's Wharf," Maggie explains as we walk briskly toward it, chattering like the children in our classrooms. At the Wharf we buy shrimp cocktails from an outdoor fish market and stroll casually through the throngs of people, studying the menus of seafood restaurants, and enjoying the colorful ambiance.

"Ghiradelli Square," Maggie commands after we've seen the wharf. "It's a few blocks down the street." The wind sweeps us past street artists offering everything from jewelry to T-shirts. We stop to listen to a violinist playing a medley of Beethoven's symphonies, and we contribute to his open violin case. We pause to watch an artist capturing a tiny blonde girl with hues of chalk and a vivid imagination. Peggy tries to make a human statue smile—unsuccessfully. (But as we walk down the street, I look back and he *waves*!)

At Ghiradelli Square, once a chocolate factory, we climb through a warren of shops, delighting in the view of the Bay from its many vistas, sharing huge, chocolate Earthquake Sundaes, and observing chocolate being made. "I love this place," I smile to Maggie, who is loading up on chocolate for the long trip home.

"Back to the van," Maggie orders when we've seen enough shops to last awhile. We're buffeted by piercingly cold winds as we exhaustedly trudge back to the parking building that now seems miles away. When we're once again loaded into the van, Maggie commands, "On to the Golden Gate Bridge." From the bridge there are breathtaking views of the bay and the city as we sweep across and survey the tiny fishing village of Sausalito, now another shopping haven. Soon we're back on the bridge, on our way to Golden Gate Park. "We'll stop for a minute at the Japanese Tea Garden," Maggie explains. "You'll love it—it's a beautiful traditional Japanese garden with tiny bridges joining a formal garden." Over tea, we delightedly share a treat of cookies and Japanese crackers. Peggy sighs, "This is just how my backyard will look someday." (We've all seen Peggy's backyard—she's got a distance to go.)

"Now the museums," Maggie offers. "For just a few minutes so you can get the feel of them."

"Could we do them another time?" Peggy asks, rubbing the sides of her head. "I'm exhausted."

Maggie smiles, shaking her head, "There's no time like the present. After all, we're already here." We scurry through the deYoung Museum and have a brief glimpse of the Natural History Museum and Aquarium. Our feet are dragging, and we're all very tired. Outside, it's turned from a windy day of brilliant sun and bright-hued sky to a late afternoon of fog drifting in with wispy, shivering fingers. "I'm starved," Mary Ann wails. (Mary Ann is always either eating or starving, one or the other.)

"Then it's definitely time for Chinatown," Maggie grins. "And I'll drive. Olivia is too polite to get a parking space."

As Maggie viciously encircles Chinatown, she suddenly leans on the van's horn. "There's a parking space," she yells, "but that car ahead of us is going to take it," she hollers, frantically motioning. "We're starving," she explains to the bewildered man who is trying to park his car, as she rolls down the window. "Move along—I have to feed these people!" The man, obviously thinking he's about to be attacked, guns his engine and takes off. After easing the van into a parking place, Maggie orders, "Follow me," as she leads us through the bustling crowds of Chinatown, down a flight of stairs to a restaurant. "Wing Chang," she smiles as she embraces the owner.

"Do you think she's ever met him before?" I whisper to Shelly.

"Maybe, maybe not," Shelly answers. "With Maggie, you never know."

But Wing Chang has risen to the occasion and finds us a paneled room to ourselves. A kimono-clad waitress pours our hot tea while Wing Chang himself prepares to take our order. "Give us your best," Maggie asserts, "These people are hungry."

Plate after plate of mouth-watering food soon arrives. Mary Ann asks, "Just what are we eating?"

"Just eat," Maggie orders. "You're too young to know."

After a filling and delicious meal, we exhaustedly arrange ourselves in the van with Olivia again at the wheel. "Now then," Maggie begins. "The view from Coit Tower is not to be missed!"

Peggy wails, "Home, Maggie. I want to go home!"

So after a detour to the top of Russian Hill where the spectacular city lies before us, twinkling with beauty, we do exactly as Peggy orders. There is a saying: "Everyone should be permitted to love two cities—her own and San Francisco." Everytime I come here, I am reminded of that.

Lord, I'm breathless both with exhaustion from Maggie's tour and with the wonders of Your creation. Bless Maggie and keep her always as she is today—and help the rest of us to be able to keep up with her—or at least not to get in her way! Amen.

A generous man will prosper; he who refreshes others will himself be refreshed. PROVERBS 11:25

THE BETTER GIRLS

I first learned about the better girls when I began teaching. It seems that the better girls set the standards for dress and behavior. Exactly who they were or how standards were set, I never determined. However, Rosemary and Grace, two fifty-something teachers at our school, were definitely better girls, because they said so.

Grace would say, "Well, I tried on a dress at Scotts', but I didn't think the better girls would wear it, so I didn't get it."

Then Rosemary would say, "The better girls are all wearing their hair this way now," as she carefully appraised her new hairstyle.

Or "The better girls go to London in the summer to see the latest plays and to shop at Harrod's." (To be most effective, this latter comment would be said with a slight, almost imperceptible, trace of an English accent.)

Of course, the better girls could not shop at the stores in our little town. Marshall Fields in Chicago was the nearest outlet for the better girls' clothing.

None of the better girls' comments affected me much until Grace drew me aside one day. "I hear you are going to Chicago this weekend," she began.

"Yes, a friend and I are going to see the musical *South Pacific*," I replied.

"Wonderful, you'll love it," she smiled. "I was wondering if you could do a small favor for me in Chicago?"

"Sure," I answered quickly.

"Well, go to Marshall Fields. On the second floor they have girdles. I'm desperate for a new one, and I wear only the better girls' clothing."

I was beginning to feel apprehensive.

"I have all the information on this card. All you have to do is to go in and find this girdle. It won't take but a minute," she finished, handing me a card with her size and the brand of girdle on it.

When we got to Marshall Fields that Saturday, I tried to saunter casually around the girdles, hoping to gracefully zero in on the better girls' sizes without attracting too much attention. Better girls, in this case, were also bigger girls. Just as I reached for the correct one, a haughty saleswoman accosted me. "Oh, honey, that girdle is not for you. Oh, my, no." She shook her head as she appraised my then-slender form. "A girdle you do not need."

"You don't understand," I stammered. "This girdle is for a friend."

She rolled her eyes in disbelief. "You're buying a girdle for a friend?"

"Yes, well, yes," I stammered.

She shook her head as she took the girdle to the cashier. "This one is buying a girdle for a friend," she sighed with exasperation.

By then I was thoroughly embarrassed. "Not too tactful, buying a girdle for a friend," the cashier scolded. "You sure you want this?"

"I'm sure." (I'd come too far to stop now.) Besides, what would Grace say if I returned home without it?

Holding the girdle out to its full expanse, she shuddered. "If you wear this yourself, you're going to get lost forever, that's for sure," she finished as she stuffed the girdle into a bag.

As I left, there was a small enclave of saleswomen staring after me, shaking their heads with disapproval.

I never bought a girdle again for the better girls or, for that matter, for anyone else.

Lord, the lesson of the girdle, I guess, is to put on the whole "armor" of God and not to worry about how our deeds are interpreted by others! Amen.

In the same way, good deeds are obvious, and even those that are not cannot be hidden. 1 TIMOTHY 5:25

MAGGIE AND THE
MOTORCYCLE

Maggie, our third grade teacher, has taught at Adams School for as long as anyone can remember. She's truly a blithe spirit, given to back flips on roller blades, vacations in the Scottish Moors, and encounters with her elderly Morris Minor. Being around Maggie means adventure. Riding with her in her car is very much akin to Mr. Toad's Wild Ride at Disneyland. So when she begins to bring motorcycle brochures to school, we are all apprehensive. "You're not thinking of buying a motorcycle?" I ask her questioningly one day.

"I'm thinking about it. I haven't done anything special for myself for a long time. I've found a great deal on a Suzuki 1100, painted red, white, and blue." She sighs with longing.

Shelly looks up from a stack of papers she is correcting. "Well, you might as well just book yourself into the hospital right now. Motorcycles are dangerous."

"No, it's just the people who drive them," Maggie argues. "I'd be really careful. You know I've never even had a ticket." Those who have ridden with Maggie know that not getting a ticket is pure circumstance. Maggie drives just sixty miles an hour, but that's at intersections in town.

One morning as I head from the school parking lot, I hear the loud whining of a motorcycle and turn to see Maggie astride a huge motorcycle, her orange curls peering out of a yellow neon helmet. She waves cheerfully as she takes the curb with a leap. "Isn't she magnificent?" she asks as she dismounts.

"I just hope you are careful," I mutter.

"Don't worry," she pats my arm. "I pray everytime I get on it. It's a whole new life. There is so much to learn!" she grins.

I try not to think about Maggie's motorcycle except when I'm praying.

Lord, Maggie is a cliff-hanger; she lives life on the brink and to its fullest. We all could use an infusion of her courage and of her ability to laugh at the challenges of life. Still, I worry about the motorcycle. Amen.

But the righteous are as bold as a lion. PROVERBS 28:1

TURKEY TALES

Every year at Thanksgiving I ask my first graders how they would cook the Thanksgiving turkey. I am always surprised.

"I know you get this barbeque sauce and paste it on the turkey. Then you put it on the barbeque for four minutes. Then add a little watermelon. Serve it with milk," George suggests.

Connie says, "First you have to look for a store. Then I'd try to find a big, big turkey. I'd carry it home and cook it in the oven for twenty minutes at ten degrees. Then I'd start to cut it up. Then I'd go back to the store and buy all the stuff that I need. Then I'd start telephoning people to come," she grins. (I hope she doesn't know *my* phone number.)

I nod to Phillip to begin. "Kill the turkey. Then put a stick through it and roast it in a fry pan. It will take thirty or forty minutes. Then serve it with carrot sticks," he finishes.

Kathy says, "Make stuffing out of bread and other stuff." She hesitates. "Grandmas are the only ones who can do it," she asserts. (She may be right.)

Michelle adds, "Get a turkey and get it all dead and stuff. Put it in the oven at five degrees for a couple of minutes. Then make sure it is really dead. Take it out of the oven and cut it in little pieces. Make corn and beans and apple juice."

Pedro, looking thoughtful, begins to speak. "Take off the beak. No one likes to eat it," he explains. "Put the rest of the turkey in the oven for about half an hour. Then let it cool and serve it with lots of salt."

"Before you can cook a turkey," adds Brandy, "you have to put A-1 sauce on it. Then lay it on the grill for an hour. Pour green beans in a bowl. Serve it with that kind of punch where you just put everything in."

"You have to cook a turkey for a long, long time," Rachel contributes. "Probably half an hour. Take it out and carve it. Mash potatoes and raisins together to make the stuffing."

Yolanda continues, "You have to get the turkey and squeeze it hard." She demonstrates, wrenching her hands. "Then you put stuff in it. Cook it for six minutes at a hot temperature. Then turn your back. Count to one hundred. Turn on the light and eat."

"I know you have to stuff the turkey with roast beef," Kari explains. "Cook it for thirty minutes or less. Take the turkey out and serve it with mashed potatoes, rice, roast beef, and pumpkin pie."

Emily nods in agreement, "That sounds good. But I'd take a knife and cut off all the fat. Start by putting the turkey in the oven for at least half an hour at ten degrees. Take the skin off the potatoes and squish them up with gravy. When it's done, we'll all have a nice dinner together," she grins toothlessly.

"Cook the turkey in the oven for one-half hour at two hundred degrees," Susan offers. "Put lettuce around it and sprinkle allspice and pepper on it. Serve it with potato chips."

"Put the turkey in the oven at two hundred degrees for five hours," Andy suggests. "Pour iced tea and green vegetables on it and serve it all with rice."

José contributes, "Put the turkey in the stove and cook it for two or three hours. Take a potato, peel the skin, and smash it. Make a salad with white stuff and add little carrots."

Mark's hand waves for attention. "I know you take a gigantic pot and put turkey in it. Throw it in the oven. Cook it for three minutes. Serve with a bowl of vegetables."

"I know how to do it," Julie interrupts. "Put the turkey in a pot. Stuff it with vegetables and carrots. Put salt and pepper on it. Put it on a tray. Then put everything in the oven for one-half hour at nine degrees."

Clay begins, "Buy a turkey at Von's. Take it home and take the package off the turkey. Cook it in the oven at five hundred degrees overnight. Squeeze out the juice and taste it. Then put some little spices on it to make it taste good," he finishes.

Every year at Thanksgiving my husband suggests, "It's so much work making a huge dinner. Let's just go out to a restaurant." Every year I decline because in my most secret heart of hearts I'm afraid that one of my first graders will have grown up, become a chef, and will use one of her recipes at the very restaurant where I'll be eating.

Lord, thank You for each of these little ones entrusted to me. Bless and keep them in Your care (and out of the kitchen). Amen.

I will praise God's name in song and glorify him with thanksgiving. PSALM 69:30

A TEACHER'S WORK IS NEVER DONE

The alarm clock blasts me out of peaceful slumber. Yawning sleepily, I reach to turn it off—5:00 A.M. Then I remember that I'm going to school early to prepare a unit on sea life. I shower quickly, don my favorite dress, and grab a banana and a glass of orange juice on the way out the door. I'll make coffee later at school.

At school, silence treads the darkened hallways as I make my way to my classroom and unlock my door. Prototypes of sea life in varying shades of bright construction paper cover my desk amidst other sea creatures awaiting completion. Fortunately, I'm a morning person, so I eagerly attack the work to be done.

Around 7:00 A.M. I decide to take a break. I make a pot of coffee from the miniature coffee machine at my desk. As I survey my classroom, I wonder what it would look like as an undersea world. Each year my class constructs a rain forest to enhance learning about endangered forests, wildlife, and plant life. An ocean should work as well. It will mean more difficult work for me, but it will also make the sea-life unit more authentic for my first graders.

By 8:00 A.M., with the clatter of an awakening school in the background, I am still sketching plans.

When the children arrive, they are as enthusiastic as I am. "It's going to be so much fun," Susan grins. The class urges me through the basics, and the pace of learning gallops rapidly through the day.

"Do we have to go home so soon?" Phillip asks at 3:00 P.M.

I nod, but I love his question! "We'll work on our ocean tomorrow," I promise. "Now it is time to clean up."

They moan and sigh good-naturedly, but their complaints are pure pleasure for me. One of the special rewards of teaching is when the children don't want to go home.

After chatting for a few minutes with Shelly after school, I'm back at my desk, still working on the sea-life unit. After awhile my muscles tense, and I graduate to the beanbag in the corner, where I spread everything out before me on the carpet.

By five o'clock I'm starved. On the way home, I stop at the market for roasted chicken, salad, and Amanda's favorite rolls. After a quick break for dinner, Jim takes Amanda to ballet, and I return to work on my unit.

"Don't you think it's about time to stop for today?" Jim suggests at ten o'clock. I nod, and over steaming cups of hot chocolate Jim and I discuss our day. I take another quick shower and am smugly asleep midway through the eleven o'clock news.

Lord, when everything is going well, there is nothing more glorious than being a teacher. Help me to store up these rewarding moments for the difficult times I know will also come. Amen.

I press on toward the goal to win the prize for which God has called me heavenward in Christ Jesus. PHILIPPIANS 3:14

THE GOSPEL
ACCORDING TO EMILY

It's two days until Christmas vacation. Intricate snowflakes nestle on a towering pine tree, and reindeer ornaments chase each other around its branches. Softly jingling sleigh bells echo on wind chimes while the fragrant aroma of gingerbread cookies permeates and lingers sweetly in the air. Glittering beneath the tree are Christmas treasures for each child and felt-stocking angels bulging with fruit and candies.

I love the frantic, festive days of Christmas. I love the tolerance we seem to develop for each other when Christmas is near. I love to see the Christmas spirit expressed in kindness and love toward others. I love the softly twinkling lights and the warm glow of a fireplace adorned with Christmas stockings. And I love the Christmas story. But I've never heard it quite in the way Emily tells it to me this year.

It's after school, and Emily has lingered. "Mrs. Fisher, can I help you?" she offers.

"Oh, tell me a story," I say.

She grins. My class this year is into stories, writing them as well as telling them.

"Well, once upon a time there was Mary and Joseph," she begins, studying me carefully. "They took a big trip," she pauses as she wrinkles her forehead trying to remember the details.

"Did they fly on an airplane?" I ask.

"No," she smiles. "They didn't have airplanes then. They had a donkey. And they traveled and traveled. When they got tired, they couldn't get a room in a motel because there weren't any vacancies."

I can tell that this is a very modern version.

"So there was this stable where they had to stay. Then Mary had a baby, and His name was Jesus. Shepherds saw a star right over His manger, and they came to see the Baby. Some other people, wise men or kings, I forget, brought the Baby gifts—gold, frankenstein, and myrrh," she finishes.

"That's a wonderful story, Emily," I tell her. I decide not to correct her account. Instead she gets a very large hug.

Lord, thank You for Your greatest gift to us—Your Son, our Savior, the Lord Jesus Christ. Help us to treasure the great moment in time when the Word became flesh and dwelt among us. Bless all Your children this Christmastide, especially a little one named Emily. Amen.

Jesus said, "Let the little children come to me, and do not hinder them, for the kingdom of heaven belongs to such as these." MATTHEW 19:14

THE DIET

I'm on a diet," Mary Ann, one of our second grade teachers, announces one crispy, cold January day.

"Oh, no," murmurs Olivia," not again!"

We've already endured several of Mary Ann's diets. There was the cottage-cheese diet, when Mary Ann would consume whole quarts of cottage cheese at one sitting. Then there was the pineapple diet, when she ate only fresh pineapple. (The success of the pineapple diet was somewhat limited by Mary Ann's inability to dissect pineapples, but maybe that was the point.) Then there was the liquid diet, when she consumed great quantities of a grainy chocolate substance. In time, however, all of the diets failed because Mary Ann loves to eat. "This time I'm on a different diet. I can eat anything I want until 4:00 P.M. After that, I can drink only water."

In the next days we see Mary Ann consume diet dinners, diet desserts, diet soft drinks, and large quantities of carrot and celery sticks. She seems to be eating almost continuously.

After school one day, I meet her in the teacher's lounge. She is eating a candy bar. "Is this part of your diet?" I ask.

"Well, not exactly," she grins ruefully. "But I have to eat lots before four o'clock or I get so hungry at night that I can't stand it. Last night I went to Joe's at ten o'clock for a double bacon cheeseburger, French fries, and a chocolate shake. I've never had anything taste so good!"

"Why don't you forget dieting, Mary Ann?" I suggest. "You could just eat lots of fresh fruits and veggies and concentrate on those while you eat regular food. Also, you could start walking or doing some other kind of exercise— eventually the pounds will come off."

"That's easy for you to say. I've got to lose twenty-five pounds so I can look good at the beach," she explains.

Mary Ann is an excellent teacher. She loves every child who has ever been in her classroom. She motivates even the most difficult child. Her classroom always boasts the best equipment and materials even though she has to purchase them herself. She's fun to be with, loves shaggy-dog stories, and has a smile that lights up a room. She's a faithful friend, a progressive teacher, an admired colleague. So I wonder why she thinks she has to be slender, too.

"You know, Mary Ann, I like you just the way you are," I say.

"If only there wasn't so much to like," she sighs as she munches another candy bar.

Lord, I ask Your presence with Mary Ann. Be with her and bless her. Help the rest of us not to be critical or overbearing but instead to surround her with love and to encourage her with understanding. Amen.

For we are God's workmanship. EPHESIANS 2:10

I'M TELLING

It's a cold, brisk winter day punctuated by recess duty. When I arrive on the playground to relieve Shelly for a break, she says, "It's bad today—everyone is having an argument about one thing or another, and I've broken up at least five fights," she sighs. Every teacher knows that some days are just like this.

As she leaves, I hear Emily yell, "I'm telling," as she rushes toward me.

Those two simple words often drive parents, teachers, and other well-meaning adults into total frenzy, so I am not feeling especially gracious when Emily tugs at my sleeve impatiently. "Lisa in the other first grade has my scarf!"

"Lisa, do you have Emily's scarf?" I ask as Lisa follows Emily to my side.

"Here it is—baby," she yells and rushes off to a swing, where she begins to taunt Emily. "Baby, baby—Emily's a baby," she singsongs while pumping her legs in the air and swinging lustily.

"I'm telling," Emily yells back to her.

"No, I'm telling," screams Sarah as she runs up to me. "Tony got mud on my new coat on purpose," she complains.

Reluctantly I first assign Lisa, then Tony, to the playground bench for five minutes of time-out. Soon I have to parole them because there are so many arguments and fights that the bench is full.

The two words, "I'm telling," continue to grate jarringly around me like stormy waves crashing against a rocky shore. Hastily flung words accelerate and echo in the air, and I long for a place of peace, of moments by green meadows and still waters.

Father, our Shepherd who always listens with unwavering patience, grant me the courage and ability to change angry words into gentle tones of caring and love. Amen.

Does not the ear test words as the tongue tastes food? JOB 12:11

THE RACE

We have three first grades this year. Robin, a newly credentialed teacher, has joined Shelly and me. Robin had gone back to school when her son was in kindergarten and had just finished her teaching credential this year. This is her first class, and she has all the expectations and concerns of first-year teachers everywhere.

"Could I see your lesson plans?" she asks me before school begins.

"You can see my plans anytime you wish," I offer. There are no secrets in my lesson plans. "You can also borrow my plans anytime you'd like to."

"How do you do discipline?" she asks plaintively. "I know you reward good behavior with super stars, but it doesn't work for me," she adds.

"Use your own system," I advise her. "That's the reason I use super stars—it works for me."

"What do you do with a disruptive child?" she asks one day after school.

"I warn him first, then take a star away and talk with him," I say. "I won't let one child destroy learning for thirty-one others and for himself as well. Try every single thing you can think of. Isolation sometimes works if your classroom has enough space to isolate anyone. But whatever discipline you use, have an overall positive plan for that child, a vision to help him turn his life around. Praise every single, positive action you see. Be tenacious and tough and loving and caring. Pray for him without ceasing. And if you don't succeed, just hang in there. You never know when you'll make a difference."

Peggy, our principal, stops me after school one day shortly after this conversation. "Robin wants to trade some students with you."

"Oh?" I ask.

She thinks you could do a better job with Timmy, Aaron, and Justin. In return she'll take Annie, Emily, and José."

I stare at her, speechless. "She wants to take three of my best students and give me all three of her difficult ones?" I ask incredulously.

Peggy nods.

"I already have Phillip, Annabelle, Conrad, and Marisa."

"I know," Peggy sympathizes. "If I approved the exchange, Annie, José, and Emily's mothers would be on my case, since each of them requested you to begin with. We can't do it. You already have a demanding group."

But still I feel guilty. I'm the experienced one—I ought to be able to do it. But deep inside me, where doubts linger, I know I've reached my limit.

"Honey, you have an extremely difficult group already," Jim reassures me that evening.

Later Robin comments to me. "I just can't keep up with you. I've tried and tried."

"We're not in a race, Robin," I answer. "My pace may be faster because I've done this for so long. You don't have to keep up. You have your own strengths. Build on those."

In January, I see Robin designing intricate paper costumes for a play she's written with her class. Her whole class seems occupied and bubbling with enthusiasm. And I know she's beginning to find her way.

Lord, as we have differing ministries and differing gifts, let us encourage one another in love. Amen.

Each one should test his own actions. Then he can take pride in himself, without comparing himself to somebody else, for each one should carry his own load. GALATIANS 6:4–5

THE WINTER PICNIC

Although most schools have cafeterias, there are those that do not or have had to convert them for extra classroom space. Those schools often have a patio with picnic benches and a patio cover so that they can be used in inclement weather. Today is inclement by any standards. Thick raindrops splatter against the canopy, while a biting wind brings an unexpected drenching to those beneath it.

This is option one. Children eat outside in all kinds of weather no matter how cold or wet. Option two is leaving children in classrooms to eat. No teacher likes either option. Most of us would prefer to have the children indoors, but we would also like a break. In any case, the choice is not ours. Peggy, our principal, has a flag for days like this. Newly designed this year, it's black fabric imprinted with white letters proclaiming "Rain" and flies from the eaves under the roof of the office. When Peggy hoists the flag letting us know that it is officially raining, she has a second flag—yellow for lunch indoors and green for lunch outdoors. No one is permitted to deviate once the flags are waving.

Merry is shivering, I notice. She has no winter jacket. Emily is back for the first day after a particularly painful ear infection. Danny has a dripping nose, and Carmen has a sore throat. Hardly anyone has the proper clothing to be outdoors in a rainstorm.

At the last faculty meeting I volunteered to keep my class in on very rainy and cold days, but Peggy had replied, "If I let one person do that, I'd have to require that everyone do it."

"Look, Peggy," Olivia had interrupted. "We're selfish— we don't want children to miss school any more than is absolutely necessary. I know some children are going to get sick after very cold or rainy days, and that directly interferes with the job I am trying to do."

"If we could just have five minutes for a restroom break and to get our lunches, I see no problem," Shelly had agreed.

"Not every teacher wants to give up a lunch hour," Joanne, one of our fourth grade teachers, had admitted.

"And that's exactly why no one is going to do it," Peggy had finished.

Still, I wonder if we could hire some parents to come in for an hour a day in the worst weather, perhaps from November through February. But I already know the answer. There are no funds for something that makes this much sense.

In the meantime, I am standing under the canopy, trying not to get wet on this stormy day because I have lunch duty. Emily and Merry are huddled next to me, shivering and watching the rain gusting in freezing sheets. "Oh, Mrs. Fisher, I'm so cold," Merry sobs.

Lord, hear my prayer for Your little ones who have no shelter from the storm. Lord, hear my prayer for Your bigger ones who cannot find a way to bring them protec-

tion. Bless all Your children as we weather the storms of life. Amen.

> I tell you the truth, whatever you did not do for one of the least of these, you did not do for me.
> MATTHEW 25:45

A REMOTE POSSIBILITY

Look at Tony," Merry whispers while we're in the midst of reading group one day.

I glance up. Tony has his head down on his desk, and he is sound asleep. When someone falls asleep in my classroom, I usually just let him sleep. After all, if a person is that tired, how could he possibly be learning anything? (Of course, I wouldn't let him do it every day.) Still, as I observe Tony over the next few days, he seems exhausted most of the time. Finally I say to him, "Are you getting to bed early at night?"

"My mom makes me go to bed at eight o'clock," he complains. "I never get to stay up late," he continues mournfully.

"Why do you think you're so tired?" I probe.

"Oh, I have to get up at five o'clock in the morning every day. It's not even light outside then," he replies.

"Does your mom have to go to work early?" I persist. Perhaps he goes to a baby-sitter before school.

"No, but I have three brothers and four sisters, and they're all older than me," he explains carefully. "So unless I get up before they do, I can never get the remote for the TV. Whoever has the remote gets to choose what to watch. So I have to get up at five," he finishes, stretching.

As we are getting ready for lunch that noon, Tony brings his lunch pail to my desk. "See," he says, "I brought the remote control to school with me. That way no one can get it." He grins with pride.

Lord, I think there's a lesson for all of us in Tony's remote. When we trust in material things to comfort us, we are going to be disappointed. But when we trust in You, You are in the midst of us as an active, caring, and personal, loving God and Savior. Amen.

He who watches over you will not slumber. PSALM 121:3

"PERVERIBLY" BAD

As we struggle with the challenges of language in our classrooms, I'm reminded of my own family. My grandparents came as newlyweds to America from Sweden. They came as far west as Illinois, where they opened a grocery store among other Swedish immigrants. Even though they continued to speak Swedish at home, my grandmother was a determined woman, and her family eventually became fluent in both English and Swedish. But not without a battle.

There were times when my grandmother's children, my mother and her siblings, were expected to speak English—at school, mainly. There was also a place for Swedish, at home, in family gatherings, and at church, where the Swedish liturgy provided a measure of comfort and remembrance in a time when everything else was new and sometimes threatening.

Goldie, my mother's oldest sister, had no problems with language. Instinctively, she seemed to know which language was most appropriate at any given moment. Without a problem she entered confirmation classes at the Swedish Lutheran Church and was able to speak her confirmation vows in Swedish.

But then it was my mother's turn. Like second children everywhere, she benefited by the experiences of her older sister. So she spoke English before she even attended school. In fact, she spoke so much English that she began to forget her Swedish.

Finally, there came a day when it was time for her, too, to be confirmed. By then, however, she'd begun to use English almost exclusively. After much struggle in confirmation class, the pastor came to call. These were the days when it was considered an honor to have the pastor come to your house. The white doilies on the living room furniture were carefully and immaculately laundered, the sofa beaten of any remnants of dust, and the whole house carefully cleaned. The air was scented with freshly baked cookies, and Swedish coffee was expertly brewed.

As Pastor Magnussen came in, he was cordially shown to the living room, where he graciously accepted a small plate of assorted cookies and a cup of coffee before he came to the point of the visit. "I have bad news," he spoke in broken English. "Your daughter, Minnie, cannot be confirmed in Swedish. She mixus the English vit the Swede, and it sounds so perveribly bad."

Years later, my mother remembered the humiliation of that moment. It was fine to speak English in school but a family disgrace when she had to be confirmed speaking English. As for Pastor Magnussen, he went on fulfilling his pastoral ministry, consuming aromatic, tasty cups of Swedish coffee and pastries until he was nearly ninety years old, combining the English vit the Swede in a way that could only be termed "perveribly" bad.

Lord, help us to speak of Your love and redemption no matter the language of our words. Especially bless those children in our classes from whom we are separated by the constraints of language. Help us to continuously and vig-

orously pursue solutions to the problems that separation brings. Amen.

Accept one another, then, just as Christ accepted you, in order to bring praise to God. ROMANS 15:7

DILEMMA

I've been up all night with my daughter, Amanda, and bronchitis. She's still barking in the background as I call Peggy. "Amanda is ill," I tell her. "I won't be there today."

"Very well," she tells me curtly, in a voice that conveys her disapproval.

A sick child is the dilemma of working mothers and fathers everywhere. Should I be at work, worrying about my child at home? Or should I be at home, worrying about my children at school? Naturally, Amanda wins. Still, I know that Peggy is affronted that this is so. I've somehow become diminished in her view. I've become someone who is not as dedicated as I should be.

At the doctor's office there are other moms and dads impatiently glancing at watches while juggling sick children. A few pace the floor, looking downright desperate. What do we do when the children are ill?

At Adams School there is one personal-leave day for each year. Sick leave cannot be used for family. I know teachers who call in sick when their child is ill. I know others who leave their child alone, risking the child's health and safety because it's so complicated and expensive to take time from work. Other teachers, having exhausted all other available options, smuggle the sick child into their own classroom, thus exposing the whole class to illness.

In a few cases, grandparents will help, and sometimes dads can take a turn. But still, it's very difficult to have both a sick child and a job. Life can be difficult and so fragile in times like these.

Lord, help me not to despair in moments when I feel tugged in all directions at once. Be with Amanda and heal her, Father. Amen.

But we have this treasure in jars of clay to show that this all-surpassing power is from God and not from us. 2 CORINTHIANS 4:7

MY GRACE IS SUFFICIENT

I've not been feeling well for several weeks. I'm always exhausted with a fatigue unaffected by rest. Shelly says to me one day as I drag into the teacher's lounge at break, "Are you sure you're all right?"

"I'm not certain whether I'm sick or well," I admit. "I just hope I don't feel like this for the rest of my life," I mutter as I collapse on the sofa, watching Shelly peel an orange.

At night I come home from school and go right to bed, but in the mornings I still feel overwhelmingly tired. "I guess I could be ill," I say to Jim one night when I awaken from a five-hour nap after dinner.

He takes out the thermometer and hands it to me. I sit there feeling slightly foolish for having made such a fuss, but when I take out the thermometer, it reads 103.9°. "This thermometer doesn't work," I tell Jim as I shake it down. So I try again to take my temperature, but the result is the same.

"What are you doing?" Jim asks as I get up out of bed and rummage through the drawers.

"Looking for another thermometer—here it is." I pop it under my tongue, but when I take it out, it also reads 103.9°.

Jim feels my forehead. "You're burning up with fever! We need to see a doctor."

"I don't want to call a doctor at this time of night," I moan. It is after ten.

"Then we're going to the emergency room," Jim says firmly. "They can find out what's wrong and give you an antibiotic and whatever else you need." I don't feel strong enough to argue, so reluctantly I pull on jeans and an old sweatshirt.

But when we get to the emergency room, the nurse does call my doctor, and I am reassured that we will get a diagnosis quickly and I can be on my way.

"Where does it hurt?" my doctor asks questioningly.

"Nowhere and everywhere. I just don't feel well," I reply.

"You'd better think about staying a couple of days. We'll run some tests and find out what this is all about," he explains quietly.

"I'll miss school," I hedge.

"You're sick," he replies.

By this time I'd been poked, pricked, and prodded. "We know it's an infection, so we'll start two kinds of antibiotics, then when we know more we'll discontinue one of them. Also you're dehydrated," the doctor concludes as a nurse inserts an IV into my arm. "We're taking you to a room now," my doctor explains as a gurney is rolled into the emergency room.

I keep wondering why I'd ever admitted that I wasn't feeling well; maybe if I'd just kept going, none of this would have happened.

Soon there are several nurses loading me into a bed. One of them begins to take my blood pressure as the doctor looks on. "It's 50 over 30 and falling," I hear her exclaim with alarm.

"ICU," my doctor orders briskly.

When I awaken, I am in ICU, and everyone seems to be scurrying around. No one seems to understand my frantic urge to communicate. Instead, a nurse pats my arm and says, "Relax now; let us take charge."

"Jim?" I ask weakly.

"Get him in here," the doctor orders.

Jim comes in quickly with both tears and love in his eyes.

"My lesson plans aren't at school," I tell him, every word thudding through my whole being.

"I'll get them there," he promises.

"You won't forget, will you? Also there's an art project in the third drawer," I finish, resting after each word, overwhelmed with the exertion of trying to talk.

That night and the next day I walked through the valley of the shadow of death. But not until my lesson plans got to school.

Lord, I wonder if when I get to heaven, will You ask, "Did you remember to bring your lesson plans?" Amen.

"My grace is sufficient for you, for my power is made perfect in weakness." Therefore I will boast all the more gladly about my weaknesses, so that Christ's power may rest on me. 2 CORINTHIANS 12:9

IN MY FATHER'S HOUSE

I am dimly aware of people around me, monitoring life-support systems. I am very tired and feel myself drifting off. The guide indicates to me that I should follow him, "I'll show you the new house."

The house sits on a bluff overlooking a sun-bleached beach. The sand is as soft as delicate white powder beneath my feet. As I wade into the ocean, myriads of brilliantly colored fish surround me in the warm, crystal-clear water. I turn to gaze at the clean lines of a clapboard gray house and climb a few steps to the polished wooden deck with intricately carved banisters and railings overlooking the ocean. For a moment I stop to sit briefly on a deck chair. Fragrant spring blossoms permeate a soft breeze.

As I enter the house, one wall is entirely of sparkling glass offering a panoramic view of the ocean sweeping against rocks below. The interior is of soft shades of wood with floor-to-ceiling bookshelves overflowing with books written by all my favorite authors. There are two softly cushioned sofas holding burly, pink-flowered pillows, and matching recliners of buttery beige leather. A blaze burns brightly in the huge, used-brick fireplace. The room is done in restful shades of blue with pastel accents. For emphasis, there are brightly flowered floor cushions propped invitingly around the fireplace.

I wander into a kitchen done all in crispy white except for French-blue tiled counters and a matching tile floor. Adjoining is a cheerful dining room with a bay window overlooking the sea. The table is of bleached soft wood-tones with a cheerful tablecloth matching the pillows in the living room.

As I peek into the next room, there is an array of desks filled with eager-looking first graders bubbling with antic-ipation. I am puzzled, and I look inquiringly at my guide. "There is still work to be done," he answers, smiling gently. "In my Father's house are many mansions."

Suddenly I am back in my bed at the hospital, and a nurse is saying, "Would you like a sponge bath?"

I nod. I am better.

Lord, help me to live a life fully committed to You, knowing that You always keep Your promises. Help me to go forward in the mission You have given me to do. Amen.

The LORD is my strength and my shield; my heart trusts in him, and I am helped. PSALM 28:7

THE SWISH OF ANGELS' WINGS

While I'm still in the hospital, I'm inundated by letters from my first graders.

Tony writes, "If yr in the hosptaal you shud no you will need money." Two quarters are taped to the letter.

Rosa moans, "It is taribul without you." She draws a picture of a little girl crying so hard that she has to hold an umbrella under her chin to catch the tears.

"I ask God to take care of you," Emily writes, "becuz the food is bad in hostils. Don't eat, Mrs. Fisher." Accompanying her letter are a dozen lollipops.

"Cum back to school," Adam insists. "We'll take care of you." Oh, yes, I'm sure they would!

"It is bad hear at school. The new teacher don't no about recess. Love Clifford." (I note with amusement that most of Clifford's problems concern recess.)

There are flowers, too—so many that there is very little room for my bed. Balloon bouquets clutch the ceiling, their ribbons waving gently.

A grubby envelope containing a single well-used balloon says, "Luv, Pedro."

Still, gifts keep arriving, mostly large boxes of candy, but from David I get a silk blouse. (I guess his mom has been shopping again!) There is a piece of wood with lots of nails hammered into it, some slightly burned homemade cookies, and a new pencil sharpener.

Katie draws a picture of me in a huge bed with angels hovering over my head. A sign held by one angel proclaims, *Head Angel*, and floating over her in a balloon is the message, "Get Mrs. Fisher well."

Tears surging, I remember how apprehensive I was earlier this year when I inherited this class. And now I feel a longing to see each one of my little ones. How could I possibly not get well with so many angels on my side? In fact, I can almost hear the swish of angels' wings.

Soon the nurses start decorating the walls with letters and pictures until every inch of space has been covered. Everyone who comes into my room says, "You must be a teacher!" When I hear those words, I know there is no greater honor on earth.

Our Father, bless these little ones; keep their faith strong, their paths straight, and if it is Your will, may I continue to minister to the children as they have to me. Amen.

The Lord is my shepherd, I shall not be in want.
PSALM 23:1

COMING HOME

It's glorious to be home. Our house is spotless, my bed freshly made with my favorite sheets. The fragrance of star jasmine covering the patio wafts through the French doors of the patio adjoining the bedroom.

Amanda says, "Is there anything I can get you, Mom?"

"Just you," I grin and hug her.

I lie down on the bed for a few minutes just listening to the birds' warbling conversations outdoors. I remember how both Kris and Jamie, my oldest two children, rushed home from out of state when I became ill and how Tricia, my middle daughter, kept things going at the house. How much of a blessing it was to have the family all together again. Then I wander through the house—touching, remembering. There's a picture of Jim and me glowing with happiness at our wedding, pictures of each of the children and one of them together, a separate photo of the grandchildren. I finger my favorite books in the bookcase. Everything is so familiar yet so new. Coming home is the best thing in all the world!

The phone rings. Amanda rushes to answer. "Mom, it's David's mom. She wants to know when to bring dinner."

"Hi," I greet her. "We can manage to do dinner—but thanks so much for offering."

"It's all worked out." she explains firmly. "Each day this week someone from school will bring dinner. We don't want you to even think about it."

And the meals do roll in day after day, meals so hardy they'd feed twenty teenagers. "I wish they hadn't gone to all this trouble," I tell Jim. "Some of these people can barely feed their own families."

Jim says, "It's your turn to accept." I do, but it's not nearly as rewarding as giving.

Our Father, thank You for Jim and the children and the grandchildren as well. Thank You for a home on earth and for the promise of a heavenly one. Thank You for first graders and their parents, for Shelly and Olivia and Mary Ann and Marty and Maggie and all the rest. Thank You for restoring my health, for all things bright and beautiful, the brightest and best of which is Your love. Amen.

No one has ever seen God; but if we love one another, God lives in us and his love is made complete in us. 1 JOHN 4:12

THE BUTTERFLY PARADE

I'm still at home, recovering, but I miss my first graders more and more each day. Now is the time they'll be growing butterflies. What a special time it is for them—how I wish I could be there. There is nothing in first grade that quite matches the high drama of new life—the day the butterflies begin to hatch. Even thinking about it brings brimfuls of tears to my eyes. My heart aches with longing. It will happen any day now. Oh, Lord, I want to *be* there.

Shelly calls me from school with excitement in her voice. "The butterflies started hatching today!"

"Oh," I reply wistfully. "I'd love to be there to see them."

Later, as I go out to the patio to sit in a lounge chair by the pool and read a book, I notice a single Painted Lady butterfly on the star jasmine covering the patio. Our butterflies are Painted Ladies, so this very butterfly could be one from my classroom! Oh, heavenly Father, I miss the butterflies!

Still later, as I look up from my book, I'm surprised to see the star jasmine laden with butterflies. And the next day and the following, everywhere there are Painted Lady butterflies.

An article in the local newspaper comments, "This city is being inundated with Painted Lady butterflies.

Longtime residents cannot recall a time when Painted Ladies migrated through our town. A spokesman at State U confirms that there is a definite change in migratory patterns this year."

A single butterfly rests on my hand, like a touch of an angel's wings. How bountiful are the blessings of the Lord!

Lord, thank You for this moment of mercy and of love. Amen.

For great is your love, reaching to the heavens; your faithfulness reaches to the skies. PSALM 57:10

BACK TO SCHOOL

I'm finally back at school, still feeling a little less than robust. I try to figure out where the class is now. Over the years I've discovered that only sometimes are a teacher's plans followed by a substitute. An enterprising substitute will, once in a while, do all the basic plans and even enrich them. Other times there's a semblance of the teacher's plans having been used, and in still other cases it's impossible to find any relationship to the plans left. My substitute was in the latter category. Everything has been changed, including the children's desks and even my own. (In fact, if I could leave a single message for a substitute teacher, it would be: Don't move the furniture!)

Then I discover a note that begins, "Your class isn't the most talented or likable class I've ever had. Still I managed to stick it out even though they were getting louder and wilder every day. You know that crystal vase on your desk? It was broken when Pedro hit Tommy over the head with it. Don't worry, Tommy's stitches will come out soon, and he really did deserve to get hit because he was teasing Pedro. Also, the globe got thrown out the window and is a little flat over China. I did overhaul your filing system and threw out the extraneous materials—they made a nice little fire in my fireplace at home. I also sent in a student book order but, by mistake, I lost the list, so I don't know what each child ordered, but I'm sure you can figure it out. Also, I didn't correct any papers while you were gone because I was sure you'd want to do it yourself, but I did get some big boxes to store them in. You'll find them stacked in the corner. If you ever need a substitute again, please think of me."

I sit down, moaning, when Shelly appears. "Why didn't you tell me?" I berate her.

"I knew it was bad, because she would yell and yell at the kids, 'How can I teach you when you won't listen?' But there was nothing you could do about it, and you already had enough to worry about." She pats my shoulder. "Don't worry, you'll get them turned around," she assures me.

For a moment tears threaten as I consider the task ahead, but then it's time to get my line from the playground. When I get there, there is a rousing cheer from all the classes and "Welcome back, Mrs. Fisher" signs waving for my attention. But my class races from the line to hug me, and before I know it, I'm immersed in a thirty-two-person hug!

Lord, how much I've missed these little faces! How grateful I am to be back. Thank You for each precious moment of teaching, because that's what teaching is—precious moments linked together to become a kind of eternal chain. Amen.

I became a servant of this gospel by the gift of God's grace given me through the working of his power. EPHESIANS 3:7

HOMECOMING

As we enter the classroom, I notice that everyone goes to his or her desk, sits down quietly, hands folded. I am amazed, but I try not to let it show, recovering sufficiently to pass out super stars, two for each child. I was fearful of rebellion and noise. But I also know the importance of expectation—what you expect is what you get. Even now, my class is deciding whether I am the same teacher I was a month ago. I have doubts about that myself. Already, fatigue is beginning to creep around the corners of my mind.

Still, the class remains cheerful and well-mannered. I think about last fall and the time and effort it took to get them this way. Now they've had a month of chaos, yet they seem much the way they were when I left. I am quietly and gratefully overjoyed. I know that sometimes when I'm not feeling my best, my class takes advantage of that. But not today. José raises his hand, "We're really good, aren't we?"

"Oh, yes," I reply. "You're the best class in the whole world," I assure him.

"Did you miss us?" asks Kenisha.

"Oh, I missed you, Kenisha and José and Lisa and Pedro...," I continue until I've included each person in the class, watching an explosion of bright smiles. It's a joyous homecoming.

Lord, I came before my class with trembling, forgetting that love and expectation cast out the darkness of fear. Let me always walk on the path that love takes, always believing that through love and faith we can surmount all obstacles. Amen.

So do not throw away your confidence; it will be richly rewarded. HEBREWS 10:35

ODE TO JOY

At last it's Easter vacation and time for a trip to Washington, D.C., to see our daughter Kris marry midst the beauty of an early spring. The day of the wedding, however, dawns with the threat of rain in the air. Randy, the groom, rushes out to rent a tent, since the reception will be held on the patio of the new house that he and Kris have purchased. Kris, checking the church one last time, discovers that flowers have not been delivered. Jim finds that his tux for the wedding has ended up somewhere in Maryland, and Amanda, fresh from the beauty shop, decides she doesn't like her new hairstyle. After several hurried telephone calls and wild car chases, we are left breathless, but all is in readiness. We're having a wedding.

Even the sun reluctantly appears, blessing the spring day with warmth. There is a virtual riot of beauty with exquisite cherry blossoms and lacy lilacs surrounding an elegantly restored colonial church. Inside, strains of Beethoven's "Ode to Joy" burst forth from Amanda's flute, both vibrant and reverent at once.

As Kris starts down the aisle, a vision in white on Jim's arm, I am overwhelmed with emotion, but my tears are pure joy that Randy and Kris have found each other to love and to cherish, to be together forever. Then Kris and

Randy move to the altar, where Jim has reappeared from the sacristy in his clerical gown as he changes roles from father of the bride to pastor, to listen to and to bless the vows. Kris and Randy look into each other's eyes, glowing with happiness, and solemnly repeat their vows.

And then suddenly it is over, and Kris and Randy stride up the aisle, smiling, arm in arm. There is a burst of "Ode to Joy" from the organ, echoing Amanda's earlier solo. I remember thirty years ago when it was Jim and I at the altar at a small inner-city church in Oakland, California, where I worked, but with the same music, the same ebullient strains. And the next year the birth of Kris—a glorious gift, our firstborn. Now, all grown, she and Randy belong together as well as to us. They're now two, to weather the trials of life and to savor its happiness.

May the Lord bless and keep them always.

Lord, bless Randy and Kris all the days of their lives and keep them forever in Your care. Bless all Your children everywhere with Your presence and Your love. Amen.

And now these three remain: faith, hope, and love. But the greatest of these is love. 1 COR-INTHIANS 13:13

THE SPIRIT OF FREEDOM

After the wedding and seeing Kris and Randy off to a Caribbean honeymoon, there is first-time sight-seeing in Washington, D.C., for us and for Amanda, our son, Jamie, and his family. It's also a time to get acquainted with my new grandson, Matthew.

It is a cold, wind-whipped day when we visit Mount Vernon to see the magnificent restoration of the estate of George Washington. A guide, clad in colonial garb, approaches us as we stand high on a bluff overlooking the Potomac, clutching each other for warmth. "You must be from California," she offers.

"How did you know?" we ask, exchanging puzzled looks.

"I can always tell a California shiver," she replies. "The sweatshirts helped, though," she grins.

We look down sheepishly at "Berkeley" emblazoned on our shirts.

Back in Washington at the mall, we take a tram to visit the monuments and museums. Our oldest grandson, Michael, at five, discovers the delights of the National Air and Space Museum, and our youngest daughter, Amanda, loves Dorothy's red shoes and has her picture taken with her favorite first ladies in inaugural gowns at the Museum of American History. I take time to add new materials for my classroom for a Washington unit. (Teachers seem to collect classroom materials wherever they go. It's second nature, a never-ending search.)

We take a quick ride by tram to the Washington Monument, echo the words of Lincoln while admiring the awe-inspiring Doric Lincoln Memorial, trace the names of young patriots who died in a place called Vietnam, and, finally, visit the columned rotunda of the Jefferson Memorial. As a light rain begins to fall, we run to the tram stop to wait for the tram to return. We huddle under umbrellas as the rain begins to fall in hearty sheets. We have a snack at the concession stand in the rain. We wait until there are more than a tramful of us eagerly searching the horizon. We call the tram headquarters. Still no tram. Finally, the tram arrives amid whistles and cheers. As we crowd in, the driver yells, "Everybody out who doesn't have a seat."

Instead, we share seats until the tram threatens to overflow. We've waited too long in the rain and aren't willing for anyone to be tossed back into the elements. Waiting has made new friends.

The driver continues, "This is the last tram today. You may get off again here at the Jefferson or at Arlington Cemetery."

A man stands, "But we didn't get on the tram here or at Arlington Cemetery. We want to be returned to where we first got on the tram, so we can get transportation."

Others vehemently nod and rise to protest. We are in the midst of a Jeffersonian standoff.

The tram guide shouts irritably, "You have a choice: Arlington Cemetery or the Jefferson Memorial."

The crowd thunders, "NO!"

"This tram is going nowhere until some of you get off! No sharing seats, either," the tram guide commands.

It is totally silent in the tram. After waiting for an hour and a half in the rain, defiance governs our little group, the silence of nonviolent protest.

We just sit there for many minutes more while the driver pretends to be busy writing a schedule.

"All right," the driver finally sighs, "I'll phone for more trams. You'll be taken where you want to go anywhere along the tram route."

We'd come to Washington to see the monuments and museums but, in addition, on a tram on a rainy spring day we saw something of the essence of democracy. We came to Washington as tourists, and we left reminded that we are the citizens of a democratic nation, knowing that our country can never be defined by monuments and buildings and cemeteries. Our government is people—people who are unafraid to stand up for justice even in a tramful of strangers on a rainy day in our nation's capital. It's a perfect story to tell my first graders.

Lord, thank You that the spirit of democracy still burns brightly in our land. May the blessings of freedom continue to echo mightily. May we always understand that freedom begins with a single person, that freedom means involvement. Amen.

But you are a chosen people, a royal priesthood, a holy nation, a people belonging to God, that you may declare the praises of him who called you out of darkness into his wonderful light. 1 PETER 2:9

PLEASES AND THANK YOUS

Back from Washington, D.C., I'm sitting at my desk, recalling my early days of teaching. It seems that children then came to school knowing more about simple rules of etiquette, like saying "please" and "thank you." Now, in self-defense, a teacher must teach a basic course of manners. It contributes to a calming environment in a classroom when good manners are part of a teacher's expectation. The simplest way for a teacher to demand good manners is to use them herself.

For example, when Tony's mom arrives with cupcakes for his birthday I will have already given my standard lecture. "What will you say when Tony's mom passes out the cupcakes?" I ask.

Kenisha's hand waves. "Say 'thank you,'" she grins knowingly.

"And what if she asks you if you want lemonade?" I continue.

José waves his hand, looking thoughtful. "Say 'yes, please.'"

"Good!" I smile. "You and Kenisha get a super star." Now every hand is up because they know there's a reward. Soon I'm giving out stars for everyone amidst a chorus of "thank yous" and "pleases."

"Now I have a really hard question," I tell them. "When you see all those cupcakes in the box or on a tray, what do you do?"

Marcus's hand is held high as he looks as if he might burst with the pride of having a correct answer. "You can look only with your eyes," he grins, "but the one you touch is the one you take."

"Wonderful!" I assure him. "What's the rule?" I ask the class as a whole.

"Look only with your eyes. The one you touch is the one you take," they reply in unison, smiling broadly with accomplishment. They're ready for a reward—in this case, a chocolate cupcake with thickly swirled chocolate icing, and a tall glass of lemonade.

"Also," chimes Kenisha, "you don't start to eat your cupcake until Tony begins to eat."

"That's absolutely correct," I praise her as I watch thirty sets of eyes riveted on Tony, waiting for him to take his first bite of cupcake.

How important is taking time from academics for teaching good manners? First, it doesn't take that much time. It blends very nicely into a few slices of time often wasted when lining up or after recess or just before going home for the day. Second, it develops consideration for others and improves the attitude of a classroom. In a world intent on violence and disruption, developing concern and caring for others is a worthwhile goal for any teacher. In a small way it changes the world for the better.

Lord, help us always to be considerate and caring of others even when there are no chocolate cupcakes! Amen.

In everything set them an example by doing what is good. TITUS 2:7

WHO'S THE BOSS?

Once upon a time when I was in an education class in college (yes, they did have colleges then), the professor said to us, "Be certain to cultivate both the custodian and the school secretary. They are the people who run the place. Not only do principals come and go, but they generally do not have a feel for the pulse of the place. By the very nature of the job, they are isolated from the rest of the school."

Also, I've discovered through the years that there are many mediocre principals. Once I worked for a principal who absconded at the beginning of March with school funds, the school car, and the school secretary. Too many teachers have had a principal who forced her to change grades because of star athletes or parental persuasion.

One principal I know walks the school track most of the day, talking to himself. (Those who teach at his school say that it's for the best!) Another principal would lock himself in his office all day. In fact, three new teachers wouldn't have been able to identify him even at the end of the school year. One principal, who was working on his doctorate, never even came to school. The school functioned very well without him.

In any case, the school custodian and secretary are right out in traffic, in the intersection of life, with the rest of us. The school secretary handles everything from playground injuries, angry and distraught parents and frustrated teachers, as well as running a counseling service, keeping the files, manning the telephone, and all the other routine activities of a secretary.

The custodian is the chief counselor for the children. The children all know his name and usually find him willing to discuss their problems. Often the custodian is the one who holds the school together by his creative efforts to repair all the many aches and pains of an aging physical campus. I knew one custodian who would cheerfully clean all the tiny fingerprints on the school's glass front door and then stand back to watch the children open the door and leave another whole set of fingerprints. Then, just as cheerfully, he would clean off the smudges again. Custodians always know the latest gossip; they are the second-best source of information about the school (the school secretary is the best).

One year I taught in a school where the principal was gone for eight-week periods at a time, never even bothering to check in. Notwithstanding, with teachers running the show, there was as much excellence in that school as I've ever seen in education. Without a secretary or a custodian, however, school could not have continued to exist even for a single day.,

Lord, I pray this day for every school custodian and every school secretary, for they also serve You. Bless their ministries and sustain them in Your love. Amen.

Make it your ambition to lead a quiet life, to mind your own business, and to work with your hands, just as we told you. 1 THESSALONIANS 4:11

TARGET PRACTICE

Adams School has an assistant administrator this year, a young man named Harvey, just out of a master's program at a state university. He has much to learn about teaching, teachers, and children, and views the world with a touching innocence and enthusiasm too rare in the world as it exists today. Happily, he does extra playground and lunch duties, which especially endears him to the rest of the faculty. He loves philosophical discussions of education along with morning coffee, and we all linger in the faculty lounge to talk with him. Peggy has a job as principal, but Harvey has a mission.

I'm thinking about how Harvey had enriched the school as I unlock the door of my classroom one morning. It's very early, and I'm the first one to arrive. I have several papers to run off, and early mornings are a good time to beat the crowd to the photocopier. As I gather up my materials, I reflect upon how quiet the school is. Suddenly I have an ominous feeling about being all alone in a creaking old building in a neighborhood that isn't very safe. I tell myself that my feelings are nonsense, that I've come to school at this time for years and nothing unusual has ever happened. But I've managed to give myself a case of the jitters, and cautiously I peer into the hallway before proceeding. I remind myself that silence and the absence of people is the reason I came to school so early. As I start down the hallway, my arms laden with classroom materials, a figure suddenly darts from the school office. The shadows of the hallway prevent me from identifying the person, but I can quite clearly see a *gun*. And it's pointed at *me*!

I hear one shot and then another as I drop to the floor, expecting to feel an onslaught of pain. Still the gun continues to fire. Suddenly there is cold silence as the figure rushes toward me in a seemingly threatening way.

"Oh, Pat, I'm so sorry," Harvey says as he helps me to my feet. His face is a vivid shade of red. He holds the gun out for me to inspect. "It's just a starter pistol for track," he confesses. "I didn't know anyone was around. I guess I just got carried away, playing cowboys and Indians," he admits with full-blown embarrassment as he picks up my papers now strewn around the hall.

I am still shaken, and my heart is pounding. It will take awhile to be amused. Harvey runs off my materials for me while I drink a cup of coffee. It was all very real for a moment. After awhile, I think of teachers who have to teach with the risk of real terror and real guns. In these times, that may be any one of us!

Lord, be with all teachers who are in fear and danger of their lives. Bless all of us in the mission You have given us to do. Guide us all in the paths of righteousness. Give us the strength and courage to serve You always. Amen.

If you make the Most High your dwelling—even the LORD, who is my refuge—then no harm will befall you. PSALM 91:9–10

MY SIDE HURTS

When my son Jamie was in third grade, he detested spelling. He'd go to any lengths to find a method of avoiding the weekly spelling test. One day when it was time for the test, he carefully raised his hand.

"Yes, Jamie," his cheerful teacher replied.

"My side hurts," he complained.

"Good thing you don't have to use it to write with," she grinned, helping him number the words.

She was two words into the spelling list when Jamie jumped up and deposited his lunch in the nearest wastebasket.

His temperature was 102° when my husband, Jim, picked him up. At home, we diagnosed his symptoms as flu and spelling, undecided about which diagnosis should be given the greater priority. He was tucked into bed, given plenty of liquids, and a dad all to himself to read all his favorite books with him.

At eleven that night he came into our bedroom. "I'm sick," he wailed, "and my side hurts."

"Your side hurts," Jim and I echoed as we exchanged panicky looks.

"Right here," he announced, pointing to his mid-tummy, right side.

After calling our pediatrician, we rushed to the emergency room, accompanied by a wary and very ill son.

"It's appendicitis, all right," the doctor pronounced as he telephoned a surgeon.

Jim and I paced and prayed while Jamie was in surgery, fearing all the things that parents fear. But by 4:00 A.M. he was out of surgery; by 5:00 A.M. he was eating Popsicles. "These are the best Popsicles ever," he'd announce cheerfully.

Within a week, Jamie was already playing football, giving a new meaning to the healing strengths of children. It took a much longer time for Jim and me to recover. Also, a third grade teacher learned that children can be even less predictable than she'd ever guessed! I regret to say, however, that he never did learn to like spelling!

Lord, thank You for being with us with Your healing hands of love when we are ill. Amen.

And prayer offered in faith will make the sick person well. JAMES 5:15A

TREASURES

Joyce, a fifth grade teacher at Adams School, collects children's books. There is one entire bookcase filled with brand-new books along with first editions and collectors' editions. Walking into her classroom and seeing all those books is total happiness, akin to getting a five-pound box of Sees Candies with chewy centers! I long for a collection just like hers! The books in my room are not nearly as extensive. What's more, my books, especially my favorite ones, are tattered with use. Favorite ones need frequent replacing even though Jim, my husband, is an expert at repairing bindings.

Once I asked Joyce how she kept her books in such good shape. "Oh," she explained, "I never let the children touch them! These are my books—my personal collection. They aren't for the children," she explains carefully.

"Well, I'm sure the children enjoy just having you read the books to them," I replied.

"You don't get it; these are *my* books, my own private collection. They have nothing to do with school."

(*Then why are they even at school?* I wonder).

How difficult it must be for the children in Joyce's room, surrounded by all those beautiful books that can never be read, beckoning to them every day. The books are a strong message to the children—"You aren't good enough to read or even be read to with new and special books." I feel sad every time I think of all those glorious books and the children who must be aching to read them.

Lord, help us to seek lasting treasures, the souls that we touch. It's as if we paint with an eternal brush, for that's indeed what we have. Amen.

For where your treasure is, there your heart will be also. MATTHEW 6:21

AN AIDE FOR ALL SEASONS

There was a time in education when most teachers had aides. This was especially true if you taught in the inner city, the ghetto, the barrio, or any other place where poverty dominated. The theory then was that children who had the least in life deserved a break; in this case, another stable adult in their life to help with language, reading, and even with new shoes or a winter jacket. The years during which I had aides were among my best in education. The relationship between a teacher and aide is an intensive kind of relationship, a friendship of shared tasks. I've probably been especially fortunate on this score—I've never had an aide I didn't like!

Perhaps that's one reason I am so disturbed when I see Martha, one of the few remaining aides at Adams School, correcting papers for one of the new teachers. A stack of uncorrected papers is an inevitable by-product of teaching, like laundry for a family. It's always there! When there's so much that it begins to climb the walls or the desk, it's time to do something about it. Leave the papers (and likewise the laundry). Martha needs to be working with a child, talking with a child, using every single moment to give a little boost to someone who cannot yet reach high enough to see out of the window of opportunity. Outside that window there's a whole new world awaiting discovery. It's true that *we don't have a single person to waste.*

Lord, help me to keep my priorities in order, people first. Sometimes it's so much easier to deal with things than with people. It's easier to do the lesser task. Help me to focus first on the people around me; help me to reflect Your love with clarity and candor now at this very moment. Help me never to put off love until another day! Amen.

But eagerly desire the greater gifts. 1 CORINTHIANS 12:31

144

THE RAINBOW

It's a beautiful spring day with birds greeting each other in song, with the scent of valley blossoms in the air, and with trees gradually donning the bright hues of the season. "Thank You, Lord," I whisper as the glorious day surrounds me and I feel new hope for all living things.

Outside the door, star jasmine covers the patio with fragrant blooms. The hibiscus has just burst into a riot of color, and soft white gardenias nestle in beds of green.

Later, at school, there's a spring shower in the brilliant sunlight. From our classroom windows we can see a soft rainbow. "Let's go outside," I suggest.

No one says, "But teacher, it's raining." (That's one of the blessings about first graders—the children still think the teacher knows best!) Instead, I collect all thirty-two of them in a happy line and watch them laugh with glee as they try to catch raindrops.

Together we watch the rainbow, and then Jorge yells, "Look teacher, there's another rainbow!" There's an admiring chorus of first graders eagerly pointing to the double rainbow, getting only a little wet.

It's a teachable moment—the moment when the time is exactly right—to introduce something new. Today it's a rainbow and a unit on weather.

We whip through the day, learning together. There are giggles and sighs of happiness, and a rainbow of promise in my heart as we finish the day with brightly painted rainbows and rainbow stories. I am at peace, in joyful communication with the Lord and with my first graders.

Lord, thank You for creating this lovely spring pageant and for inviting me to attend. Thank You for the breathtaking beauty, for rainbows, and for spring showers, and for the eagerness and enthusiasm of first graders. Amen.

Great is the LORD and most worthy of praise; his greatness no one can fathom. PSALM 145:3

GOOD HELP IS HARD TO FIND

Someone has mixed all the blocks, legos, unifix cubes, and all of the other wooden and plastic manipulatives used for building, counting, and endless other activities. It's quite a chore to sort them again, but Kari, Melissa, and Jenny are finished with their work so I enlist their assistance. Actually, I also forget them until we are getting ready for recess. "Where are Kari, Melissa, and Jenny?" I ask.

"Oh, they left a long time ago," replies Lisa loftily.

"They left?" I ask her, looking around expecting to see them any moment.

"They took all the blocks, too," she replies, shrugging her shoulders.

Quickly I line the class up for recess and trust them to find the playground by themselves. I have to find the missing ones.

As I stop in the office, there they are with all the blocks and cubes scattered over Liz's desk.

"What is happening?" I demand.

"These girls came in and said they needed my help," Liz comments, looking very puzzled.

I look at the three culprits as sternly as possible, considering that I'm ready to burst into laughter. "Whatever made you come to the office?" I ask.

"It was very hard to sort these blocks," admits Melissa.

"So we thought we needed help," adds Jenny, appraising me carefully.

I don't want to know any more. I ship my three mischief makers out to recess and then throw the blocks randomly into the box. Once again I remind myself that if you teach first grade, good help is hard to find.

Lord, thank You for the knowledge that Your help can be counted upon for our every need, even when those around us fail to meet our expectations. Even when we fail to meet our own expectations, we know that we can always turn to You, our faithful Friend and Savior. Amen.

Our help is in the name of the LORD, the Maker of heaven and earth. PSALM 124:8

JUST LOCK UP THE BOOKS

There was a time about twenty-five years ago when the prevailing educational philosophy was that young children should first learn to interact with other children before any academic skills were introduced. This theory claimed that academic skills and social skills were two separate entities. Those embracing that theory often concluded that age eight is an excellent time to begin to read—after children had learned to love one another. I could always visualize children standing in a circle with love floating around in helium balloons.

Unfortunately, it was during this time that Kris, my oldest daughter, first went to school. She'd already taught herself to read and had been patiently reading Dr. Seuss to her younger siblings for the past couple of years. I'd never imagined what kind of problems that would cause her.

After two weeks in kindergarten, her teacher called me. "Did you know that your daughter already knows how to read?" she demanded.

"Uh, yes," I'd replied uncertainly.

"We are NOT doing reading now," she exploded. "You'll have to stop her. I'd suggest you put all your books away, and also don't let her watch television. I think, that way, she'll lose interest in reading. Then later, when the class is ready to read, she can be taught in the correct way."

I stumbled through a few sentences and hastily hung up the telephone.

The next day Kris had a new teacher, who thought it was fine that she knew how to read. "One less for me to teach," she'd grinned.

As I observe teachers today, I cannot help but think of how teaching philosophies have changed for the better.

Lord, help us to love more freely, to teach more effectively, and to understand that love is most succinctly defined in context. Help us to understand that love does not drift about aimlessly but is seen most clearly in the life, death, and resurrection of Your Son. We have the example of Christ ever before us—let us never waver from His example. Amen.

The wise in heart are called discerning, and pleasant words promote instruction. PROVERBS 16:21

POMPEII OR WORSE

Some teachers leave papers and crayons and pencils strewn all over the floor. They don't even try to have their classes pick up the room. It makes so much extra work," moans Butch, our custodian, as he prepares to vacuum my room. "Your room is always ready to clean," he offers.

"Oh, but it's a challenge," I tell him. "Some days I feel like leaving everything. I'm so tired that I just want to tell the children to go home, to forget about cleaning up," I sigh. "But I always have a couple of floor monitors, and they usually take care of the floor."

Sometimes I get so tired of being positive—"Oh, I love the way Susan has cleaned up around her desk." And, "Jorge, you're doing such a good job." The very worst thing about praise is that it seems to take such a long time. The very best thing is that it works! Eventually all the children will scurry around the floor and crawl under their desks to pick up the smallest scrap of paper. Other students will clean the bookcases, carefully putting all the books in order (backward, of course). Someone will even get a dust cloth and enthusiastically begin to dust. Occasionally a child will say, "What about your desk, Mrs. Fisher?"

"That's off-limits," I tell them. Teachers' desks need to be cleaned only once a year, or when everything on the desk collapses, creating a modern-day Pompeii. Whichever comes first.

Lord, help me to keep my priorities straight. A clean classroom is a pleasant adjunct to learning—but my purpose is much more than that. Even in moments of catastrophic clutter, let ideas rule this classroom. Let grace reign. Let laughter and giggles prevail. Let love smile upon these little ones. Let adventure thrive. Let all that we do, bring favor and delight in Your sight, heavenly Father. Amen.

Let us throw off everything that hinders and the sin that so easily entangles, and let us run with perseverance the race marked out for us. HEBREWS 12:1

I'VE NEVER BEEN SO COLD

It's the end of May when Peggy organizes a field day at Adams School. This means that we'll all get out on the school track and compete for ribbons. Before field day teachers are supposed to have divided classes into "competence groups." That's administrative jargon for ability grouping. "After all," Peggy asserts, "we do want each child to take home a ribbon."

I'm in charge of the 50-yard dash. I've been given a stopwatch, an assortment of ribbons, and a section of the track to supervise. But it's not a very warm day. Usually at this time of year in the Valley we can count on temperatures in the high 80s or 90s. But today the winds seem wintry and intense, and rain is threatening. I have on a lightweight outfit befitting the season but not the day. The children, decked out in summer shorts, hug themselves and shiver.

At first I am very resolute and conscientious about handing out ribbons and timing the races. Then Liz, the school secretary, comes out with a note from Peggy. "You are really out in the south forty," she sympathizes. "You are not going to like this note."

Peggy writes, "We are running behind on races. However, we will be able to complete our agenda if we continue through the lunch hour. A cafeteria lunch will be sent to you at your station. The children will have lunch as they do the long jump."

I study Liz for a moment. "I knew you wouldn't like it," she sighs.

"I'm freezing," I admit. "And I need a break."

As Liz leaves, I tell myself that only a teacher would be expected to juggle a cafeteria tray of spaghetti, a fistful of ribbons, a stopwatch, and thirty children all at once. I long for hot chocolate with marshmallows, my quilted robe, a huge pillow, a blazing fireplace, and solitude. I've never been so cold!

Oh, Lord, You who are the Great Teacher, grant us courage and strength to meet the challenges of teaching, to overcome the obstacles, and to continue to love unconditionally. Amen.

Blessed is the man who perseveres under trial, because when he has stood the test, he will receive the crown of life that God has promised to those who love him. JAMES 1:12

FINALE

It's the last day of school, a beautiful June morning with the leafy trees whispering sonnets of early summer, and with fragrant blossoms dancing in the gentle breeze. It's a poignant time, a time to say farewells. How much I dreaded getting this class—yet what a blessing they have been to me. To think I could have missed all these blessings! How much I feared I could not instill a new image within them. How much I feared that they could not learn, or even worse, would not learn! Although it took some persuasion, they've all come along for the concert. The symphony is strong. It will never again sound exactly as it does today, but encores will echo through the years.

There is so much to *remember*:

Maggie's bagpipes and tam-o'-shanter, her motorcycle, and frenetic tour of San Francisco . . .

David's new jacket, his homework-eating dog, and his mom's shopping ventures . . .

The happiness of the wedding . . .

Harvey and his game of cowboys and Indians . . .

Letters from angels . . .

The new grandsons . . .

The day the "creek" overflowed and countless trips to Sam's Gas . . .

Clifford and his encounter with the pencil sharpener
. . .

And so much more. . . .

The music continues as I remember ponytails and freckles, giggles and laughter, small hands grasping mine, the miracle of learning to read. All that has made up this school year is now woven into an intricate tapestry of memory, a symphony of love.

Lord, thank You! My basket of blessings overflows! Amen.

"Test me in this," says the LORD Almighty, "and see if I will not throw open the floodgates of heaven and pour out so much blessing that you will not have room enough for it." MALACHI 3:10